# Feed My Sheep

### By

### Terry Cummins

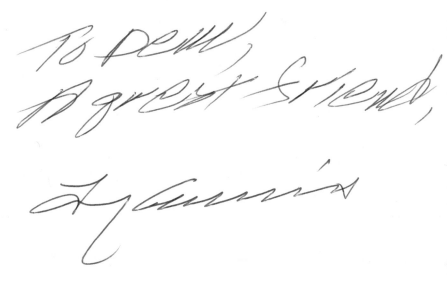

This book is basically an account, in part, of events during 1947. Some of the names of actual people have been changed.

ISBN: 1-4107-5082-5 (e-book)
ISBN: 1-4107-5083-3 (Paperback)

This book is printed on acid free paper.

The front cover photo is my granddad and me plowing the garden in early spring a few years ago. If you've got good horses, they're not hard to drive.

1stBooks - rev. 10/21/03

## Dedication

For my family, who gave me everything. Also to the memory of my farm family including Crit, Sollie, Lady and the lambs.

"He saith unto him the third time, Simon, son of Jonas, lovest thou me? Peter was grieved because he said unto him the third time, Lovest thou me? And he said unto him, Lord, thou knowest all things; thou knowest that I love thee. Jesus saith unto him, Feed my sheep."

St. John 21:17

Acknowledgments:

Thanks to Kay and Ron Swift and Bettye Weber, who read all or parts of the manuscript, and encouraged me to continue. Thanks to Cathy Kiebler, who provided valuable insight and criticism into the structure and content of the book. A very special thanks goes to my editor, Tiffany Taylor. The value of her help and assistance was immeasurable. Her painstaking scrutiny and thoroughness brought the bits and pieces into a whole. Early on, when the writing and completion were in doubt, she provided the inspiration to sustain me to the end.

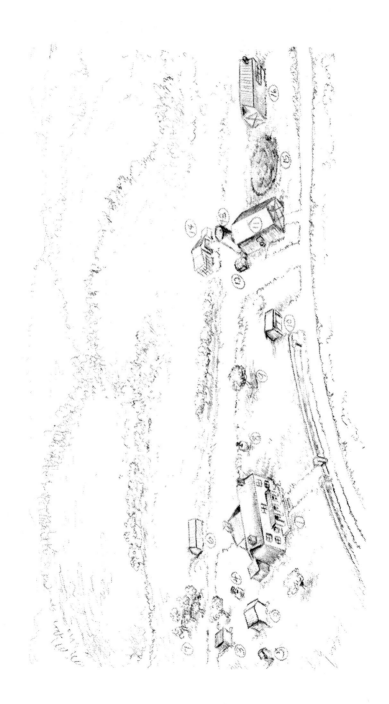

Guide:

1. This is our house, which was built around 1888 by my great-grandfather after he fought in the Civil War. The rock wall is down in front by the road. I could never draw very well, so I got a relative who can to draw pictures of our farm so you can see how it is laid out. It's all a nice place.
2. Smokehouse, where we cure our meat.
3. Wood house to keep our cooking wood dry and to keep our dogs when they're not running loose.
4. Cistern.
5. Outhouse.
6. Chicken and brooder house.
7. Fruit trees.
8. Another cistern.
9. The old pear tree, where we sit in the summer.
10. Garage with the mailbox at the side.
11. The big dairy barn, where we milk the 20 cows. It also has seven stalls for horses, sheep and dry cows, which quit giving milk a couple of months before they give birth again. The hayloft is up above and holds many, many wagon loads of hay. You can also see my basketball goal on the side.
12. The milk house where we keep about five or six ten-gallon cans full of milk overnight so Pete can take them to the city the next morning.
13. The tall silo we fill every fall with sweet smelling corn stalks cut fresh from the field.
14. The corn crib and tool shop.
15. The pond, which has catfish in it.
16. The tobacco barn, which holds about five acres of tobacco hanging up in the rails. The stripping room is where the windows are. We also have two other barns back on the place where we also hang tobacco and put up hay.

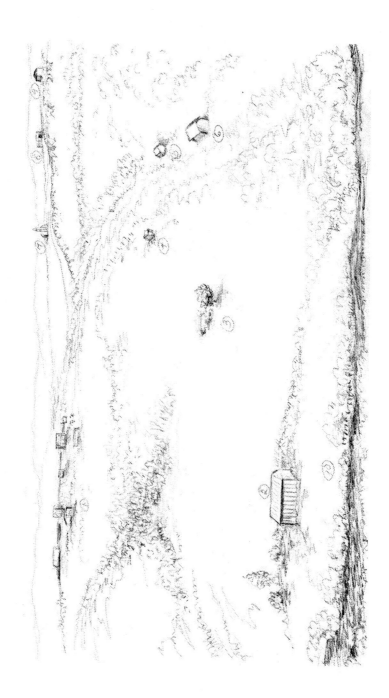

Guide:

1.  He drew this picture from the back of our place, which is spread out over 444 acres. Our house and buildings are over across the way.
2.  Our barn, two hollows over from our house. When we hang tobacco or put up hay there, we sometimes take a cooked bucket of beans, potatoes and biscuits to eat for dinner.
3.  The old pear tree and cistern where Joe Hand's house was after he was freed from slavery.
4.  Crit's three-room house.
5.  Sollie's four-room house.
6.  Another one of our barns.
7.  The Short Creek Baptist Church.
8.  Elmer's store.
9.  The Goforth Grade School.
10. The beginning of Short Creek at the back of our farm.

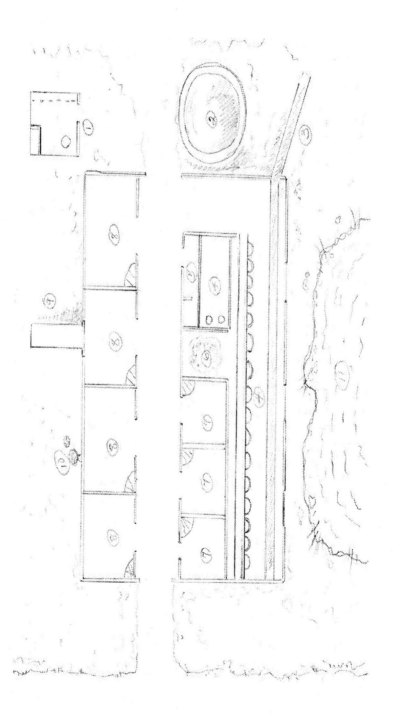

Guide:

1. The milk house. When I was little and before I started milking myself, I had to carry the buckets of milk to here and pour it into ten-gallon cans.
2. The silo. The cows really like silage to eat.
3. The manure ramp to haul out the cow manure with a wheel barrow.
4. The cow stanchions. The half circle places all lined up is where the cows put their heads and are locked in while we milk them. Some of the cows have a favorite stanchion. Old Kicker always rushes in and takes the last stanchion. She is a nervous cow.
5. The harness room.
6. This is where the hay lands when I throw it down from the hay loft.
7. Stalls for dry cows, sheep and horses.
8. Bigger stalls mostly for horses. When we bring all our sheep in to sort, castrate or doctor, we fill all the stalls up. It's a confusing place when the lambs get separated from their mothers.
9. Loading chute for loading cows or sheep to take to market.
10. My basketball goal with a ball headed toward it. I can hit it pretty good.
11. The pond. All the animals go to the pond first when we drive them in from a field. In the hot summer, when the horses have been working all morning, they drink and drink when we bring them in at dinner time. The ducks and geese stay out around the pond. I catch a few catfish at the pond now and then. In winter, I like to skate around on it.

## PROLOGUE

He was near the end of his life on earth. He lay in a hospital bed ravaged with cancer. His voice box, filled with tumors, had been removed a couple of years before. He had then received a new device powered by flashlight batteries that he could hold to his throat and use it to project strange-sounding words. It was a miracle for him at the time to be able to communicate again. But now he was too weak to speak and there was no miracle in the offing. I sat with him all through the night before he died. It was difficult to know what to say to him. I knew he wanted to speak to me, but he couldn't. There were only faint messages from his eyes. They were eyes that once looked out over the hills and valleys of his farm, and at the crops he had planted and the animals grazing in the fields. They were eyes that were always receptive to all that he observed. He could now speak only through his eyes. They revealed pain, alarm and struggle. Long ago, they spoke only of an inner peace and a tranquil radiance that connected him to all that was around him.

He spent a long life as caretaker and caregiver to the land, the animals and the people who lived with and near him. He worked for his country and community. His life efforts were in a sense instinctive. Not only did he arduously work to preserve his farm and his way of life, he always sought to improve and enhance all that was around him.

He liked most of all to be with his sheep and to watch them and care for them. He would ride out nearly every day on his saddle mare, Lady, sit up on a high ridge and look out at them. When they saw him, they would usually wander toward their shepherd. They knew he would protect them and feed them. His eyes revealed a strength that sustained him when keeping watch over his flock.

He was my grandfather, who raised me. I'm unsure whether it was his choice to undertake this burdensome but noble task, but I certainly had no choice in the matter. When I was two and a half years old, my mother divorced my father, and took my younger sister and me back to the Kentucky hill farm where she had grown up. My grandfather lived there alone in the big old two-story farmhouse. My grandmother had died several years earlier, and his three children, a son and two daughters, had gone their separate ways upon growing into adulthood.

Taking on the responsibility of raising another family must have been problematic to him, but I never sensed that he was displeased with the circumstances. As I grew and developed, his profound influence undoubtedly shaped what I was to become. He was a strong man, although his physical strength and stamina during his later years was gradually and significantly reduced. But his strength of character, uncompromising will and sense of purpose remained and were revealed in all that he did. It was a kind of strength that seemed to blend naturally with all that was around him, and in turn, strengthened those who were with him.

The forces of nature and of life take us with them. Growing up on a hill farm in the 1940s before mechanization was extremely hard. Working with the earth, the natural forces and doing nearly everything by hand to scratch out a meager living took its toll on the body, but it also tested the spirit. It was continual struggle. Most days were a test of the limits of physical endurance. And yet, to be in nature, to feel the stings of sun and wind and rain and snow, to plant a seed, to nurse a lamb, to sing in harmony with the bird songs and fill the lungs with a fresh-spring air sustained, renewed and nourished the soul.

I watched him hold to his last few hours. What could I say or do? I would talk to him, and search for words of comfort, but there were no such words. I'd ask if he wanted water, remembering the many times we drank cool, clear spring water from an old tin can at the edge of a hay field or tobacco patch. We would lie down on the shady grass by the little pool that came trickling fresh and pure from the earth where we worked. Now in the sterile room, he would gently rustle the sheets while trying to move away from the pain, and hold out his hand and I would take it. His hands were hard and drawn, revealing the story of his years of labor with an ax, a hoe, and many other tools. My granddad lived with and by his hands, but these aging claw-like hands could do a tender thing. I could see him gently hold a new-born lamb, lying in the sleet or snow and wet with afterbirth. It would be limp and near death, but he'd rub it gently with a hand full of hay or a gunny sack and dry it and send the life from his hands to the lamb. He knew how to sustain life so quickly and bring the lamb to its mother's milk and when to leave the two alone to make it through the night.

He'd given so much to life, and now this night, his life was leaving, his hands never to rub life into another creature again. I sat and hazily dreamed and thought of that year when he was strong and when I was trying to become a man of strength, like him.

I left the farm to go to college in 1952 and never returned, except for summers to help tend the crops. My sister Ann married at age 18 in 1954, and she and her husband Tommy lived with my mother and granddad on the farm. Tommy raised a tobacco crop, helped take care of the stock and maintained the farm. When my granddad became unable to care for his sheep as he saw fit, the flock was sold in 1957. My granddad was born on October 19, 1885 on the same farm, which he later purchased from his family. He died on October 13, 1961.

When he would move ever so slowly in the bed and struggle so feebly against the odds, I'd speak to him again. His eyes would tell me that he understood, and I'd take his hand. I don't ever remember holding his hand before, but noted a final strength, a final grasp of holding on. It seemed to be a plea against the obvious fate. Or perhaps it was his way of saying, "You too can feed my sheep."

We could only wait out the night. The pain and weariness during this long night were taking their toll. And then I remembered and said to him, "Tommy is getting some sheep to put back on the farm."

His eyes began to speak. His sunken cheeks and temples seemed somewhat full again. But it was his eyes. The light again began to shine. He nodded and a little feeble smile appeared. The sheep would graze the hills again, and he would be among them. He lay back on the pillow and closed his eyes. The peace that had always been with him returned.

In the stillness, I lay back in the chair and closed my eyes. And though awake, the dreams began. It was a summer and we roamed the hills together. Riding out on Lady, he would send me through the brush to get a stray. My lanky legs carried me over many a hill. He had to keep the flock together through the seasons. He sheltered them from winter storms and bound their wounds and when he called them, they would follow. He'd take a big bucket filled with grain to the trough, and they would cry and squeeze against his legs. He fed his sheep. It made the day complete.

It was in early January of 1947 in the midst of lambing time. It was soon after the war, and the times were good again. I was going on 13, a time between boy and man. I wanted to become a man, and yet I didn't. The conflict was that a boy finds the innocence of boyhood has merit over the responsibilities of manhood. In those times and circumstances, a boy was pushed, perhaps forced into carrying a heavy load. There was no waiting period. It was, however, the time I became consciously immersed in all those forces — birth, growth, labor, cultivation, creation and death — which are the natural manifestations of the cycles of life. I worked with men and was expected to perform near the limit. It was a good life and a hard life. What made it hard was that a 12 year-old was expected to fork almost as much hay as a strong man could in a hot, dry field. The good part is difficult to explain. During his last night, I realized he lived life for the good, because a shepherd has no purpose other than to tend his flock.

His last breaths seemed to mimic the wind on a long past cold winter day. I remember going out over the wind-swept ridge with him and watching as he knelt down by the frozen dead lamb ...

# CHAPTER ONE
## SAVE EVERY LAMB

My granddad took his well-worn pocketknife out of his overall's pocket, pulled out the largest razor-sharp blade and slid it under the dead lamb's skin. A cold sleet beat against the hill and against our faces as his claw-like hands sliced out a section of cold and slimy wool-covered skin from the lamb's back and sides. He needed a portion of the skin large enough to be tied over the back of a live lamb. My granddad knows how to save most every lamb. Some didn't make it, but he always does his best to keep even the frailest ones alive. For some reason known only to him, he seems to care for his sheep more than any of the other animals on our farm.

As he finished slicing out the section of skin from the dead lamb, the mother ewe circled him and shuffled about with great alarm, bleating a mournful cry. Her newborn lamb had died during the cold night, or was dead upon birth. She had not been able to bring life into its frail weak body by getting it quickly cleaned of the afterbirth. She had not been able to get it on its wobbly legs and upright in order for it to suckle its first life-giving nourishment.

The wind blew across the ridge as the dark gray clouds sent sharp pellets of sleet toward the crumpled grass stems and the brittle dried leaves. Most animals will seek some natural shelter when giving birth. This ewe had found a small buck-brush thicket under the hill and away from the strongest winds, but it was not enough. Some newborn animals will survive the severest weather. Nature is strange that way. Life or death seems to be such a chance.

My granddad wiped the blade on his pant leg, folded the knife, and slipped it into his pocket. "Throw that dead lamb in a holler and bring those other yohs to the barn," he said as he disappeared up over the ridge. He pronounces "ewe" as "yoh," and many other words in a peculiar way. He didn't have much education, but is smart about many things. He always seems to be thinking. He thinks about important things that will make our lives better on our farm. He wants to make all lives better, all the animals and particularly his sheep.

1

He picked up the cold, soggy lambskin and started for the barn. The mother ewe followed him and continued bleating in an anxious way. I felt sad for her, because she didn't know what to do.

I stood over the dead lamb, but didn't want to look at it. The only sound was the mournful cry of the mother ewe. She then began running back and forth from my granddad, as he headed to the barn with the skin, to the carcass near where I stood. She finally ran to him as the sleet began beating down again against the side of the hill. It was a soft sound at first, but then it turned to ice and began to hit with greater force as the wind drove the frozen pellets across the ridge and sent them glancing and bouncing to the frozen earth. I stood with my face away from the stings of the sleet, and hesitated to look at the skinned dead lamb. I didn't want to touch it, but knew I had no choice. I always do whatever my granddad tells me.

When stooping to lift the lamb, I caught a glimpse of its face, and wanted to think it was only in sleep with pleasant dreams. The pure white fleece around its head would keep it warm, I wished.

My granddad would be waiting, and the other sheep were waiting too. I grabbed one of the dead lamb's legs and lifted it from the ground. I looked away as I slung it with all my might down the hill. The cold blood and slime flew in my face. My granddad's hand was bloody too, but he had work to do, and his hands were often covered with dirt and mud and stains that a farmer can't avoid. I wiped my face with my coat sleeve, and then moved toward the other sheep to drive them to the barn.

My granddad seems old to me. He's 61 years old and doesn't do the real hard work like he used to do. He has arthritis in his hands and his fingers are all drawn up like claws. They're harder than tough leather, and his palms are callused and as rough as a gritty rock. He has one finger that was ground off down below the nail when he got it caught in a gristmill. If you saw him, you would take notice of his hands, because they show he's spent many years gripping an ax, hoe, shovel, hatchet, pitchfork and plow handle. He never shied away from taking anything in his hands. When a cow is having trouble giving birth, he'll stick his hands right in and help bring the calf out to life. Mud, slime, blood and manure don't bother him. Most splinters and thorns break against his tough old skin. His hands tell so much about his life.

He has a little hole in the skin in his temple. When I was little, it always made me wonder when he would laugh and say that he was shot there. One of his hunting friends mis-aimed when a covey of birds flew up, and some of the shotgun pellets hit my granddad in the face. He keeps his bald head covered, except of course in the house, at a meeting or at church. He wears an old felt hat in winter and a straw hat in summer. He gets a new straw hat every spring, and it looks like a fodder shock by the time fall rolls around. In late summer, his forehead about halfway down has become about as brown as an acorn ready to fall, but his bald head remains white and shiny year round. His nose is pretty big, as are his ears, but you don't notice them too much. What you notice more, besides his hands, is the way he acts. He always acts like he is serious about everything, and is sure of what he's doing. Oh, he laughs and likes to be sociable when he meets with a neighbor or at a gathering, but whatever he says, it is usually about making things better in the days to come. Sometimes, I get real tired of having to do everything he says, but he makes me think he knows what's best. It's hard to describe him, but I'll just say he seems to know how things all fit together.

He opened the barn doors, and I drove the sheep in. We keep our sheep in the tobacco barn during winter nights when the ewes start lambing. Our big tobacco barn is just beyond the pond that is between it and the dairy barn. We also have two other barns back on our place. My granddad often gets up in the middle of the night, lights a lantern, and goes to the barn to check on any ewe that might be having trouble in giving birth. If one of the ewes seems to be having trouble, he takes it into the tobacco stripping room at the corner of the barn and builds a fire in the wood stove. The stripping room is where we strip the dried leaves from the tobacco stalks in the winter. We need a wood stove there, because many cold days are spent standing at a long wooden bench and pulling and tying the long brown leaves into bundles, or hands as we call them, in preparing the tobacco for market. We call it stripping tobacco, and I'll tell how we do it later.

My granddad tries to save every lamb, because every lamb, except those we slaughter for meat, will be sold in summer, which is so important to our livelihood. But I also think my granddad likes to save every lamb, because, mainly, he just likes his sheep most of all. He spends so much time with them, and rides out nearly every day in the summer on Lady to check on them. He stops the mare at the top of a ridge and calls for his sheep: "Sheepy, oh sheep, sheepy, sheepy!" His voice is husky and coarse, but this long, loud call is high-pitched like a woman singer. When they come running to him from the shade of the bushes, he just watches them and studies them, and sits there still-like as they gather around him. He often has me go with him so I can run after strays, or help herd them if we are changing pastures. I get impatient waiting, while he sits on Lady looking at his sheep. I get fidgety, and sometimes pick up a rock and try to hit a tree trunk, and "nail the runner at the plate." But he taught me early on not to spook the sheep. He always has me be gentle around them. He is a rough man in many ways, but he knows how to gain trust with his sheep, so they will follow him. I think he always feels he needs to help those creatures, which are so innocent and defenseless and need help the most.

The mother ewe, whose lamb had died at birth out on the cold ground, followed him anxiously and bleated with alarm as she scampered about. She could smell the newborn scent from the skin he held in his bloody hands, but didn't know what to do.

"Help me get this yoh in the stripping room," he told me.

The fire in the stripping room stove had not gone completely out. Crit and Sollie had been stripping the leaves from the tobacco crop. Crit and Sollie are our tenant farmers living on our place, and we couldn't get along without them. They were now milking at the dairy barn as the last light from the day seeped through the cracks of the barn. After we shoved the ewe into a small pen, my granddad took a lamb from another small pen, and with twine began tying the skin of the dead lamb over its back. This lamb had lost its mother, and we had kept it alive with warm cow's milk with a rubber nipple on an old Pepsi bottle. When the skin had been tied over its back, my granddad put it into the pen with the ewe. The ewe became excited and lunged against the gate and butted the little lamb with her head. He then tried calming her by talking to her and rubbing the thick wool on her back.

"Here now sheepy, here's your lamb, here's your lamb, here sheepy."

As the ewe became somewhat calm, he put the lamb near the ewe's nose. She began sniffing it, but was still very confused. She wanted her lamb, and certainly wasn't sure that this strange looking

4

creature was hers. In time, with his talking and stroking, she settled down, and began to sniff the tied skin on the lamb's back.

He knew just when to put the lamb's mouth to the ewe's teat. He knew so many things about nature. The new lamb began sucking the milk from the ewe, but he had to hold her against the pen, because she was still uncertain and scared. At times, she jerked away and he would put pressure against her side with his leg.

"If she'll let this lamb suck, he might make it. Most all of em will make it if they can get the first suck," he said. He didn't talk to me much when working, but he told me the things he wanted me to learn. He had told me before that a ewe's milk at birth contains all the richness and nourishment that a lamb needs to survive the first few hours. After the bag is emptied the first time, the milk is still nourishing, but is not as potent with such life-giving force to a frail, weak lamb fresh from the womb.

"Go get a little crushed corn, some water from the pond, and bring some alfalfa," he told me.

He had done all he could for his sheep. The mother ewe had lost its lamb. Another lamb had lost its mother. He knew that nature allows for other ways when life is near the line of death. He knew how to work along with nature and help its course, and nature must have understood something about him.

I returned with the feed and water. He had moved the lamb back into its pen next to the ewe. The ewe was much calmer, and would rub against the wood rack and sniff at the lamb. The fire in the stove had partially dried the ewe's coat of wool and our winter work coats as well. He put the corn, hay and water before the ewe and she began to eat.

"She might claim this lamb," he said.

I knew that he would check on her and all the others sometime during the night. Some nights, I would hear him walk down the stairs, close the door and head for the barn. Lambing time was so important.

"Let's go help finish milking," he said, and we walked through the maze of ewes and lambs in darkness. When he latches the barn door, he always pauses outside and listens for a moment. It seems the sheep know when he will be gone for awhile. They stop the scurrying about and bleating and calling out for their young and each mother soon has its young beside her. If a lamb is lost in the flock, the mother begins

5

calling out and rushing about sniffing every lamb until it finds its own. The most confusing time is when the ewes are given grain or hay. Most every lamb is then separated from its mother and is crying and scampering about. The barn is filled with noise. After hurriedly eating, the mother then begins to baa and baa and go seek its own. They get very anxious as they rush to a lamb, sniff, and then go on to the next one, but all seem to get sorted out after a while. Sometimes my granddad says, "No, it's that lamb over there." I can never understand how he so often knows which lamb belongs to which ewe.

After the first of every year when lambing season comes, I'll hear him tell a neighbor or someone at Elmer Perry's store or at church that he sure hopes to get "a lamb and a half to the yoh this year." Of course, a higher number of lambs means a few more dollars when they are taken to market in the summer. The few more dollars will help make the farm payment and pay the taxes. About half of the ewes have one lamb and the other half have two, and if most are saved, then it averages around a lamb and a half per ewe. Occasionally, three are born to a ewe. When this happens, the mother can't give enough milk to support three. My granddad then has to try to get another ewe with only one lamb to claim the third lamb. Sometimes it works. But sometimes a ewe does not give enough milk for two, and a similar thing happens. On occasion, a mother won't even claim her own lamb, which seems a strange way with nature. My granddad will get disgusted and tie the ewe to a gate and help hold her while its lamb sucks. Usually, the ewe finally decides to claim her lamb. Some of the lambs that are not getting enough milk, especially those a week or more old, learn to steal milk from other ewes. They become strong little rascals, and are fun to watch. They sneak up on a ewe and begin sucking. Once the ewe realizes it isn't her lamb after sniffing it, she turns and butts it away. A few swallows of warm milk are enough for the moment, and the rascal goes on and seeks another. Feeding time, though, is the best time for this type of thievery. The ewe is busy eating from the feed trough. Lambs normally suck from the side of the mother with their little tails shaking like a willow limb in a strong wind. The sharp little thief sneaks up from behind, drops down on its front knees, sticks its head between the ewe's hind legs, and gets its dinner. The ewe is also getting her dinner and is not as concerned with what is happening at her behind, and often does not take the time to smell the suckling lamb to see if it is her own.

If a lamb isn't getting any milk for any reason, we have to use cow's milk and bottle-feed those that can't make it. This takes a lot of time, but we never let one just die away without trying something. Several times during a lambing season, my granddad will find a lamb that is nearly frozen or sick with the scours or one that has been trampled or butted too hard. He brings it to the house, rubs it with dry rags and puts it in a box by the fireplace. He then tries to get some warm milk down its throat. Usually, the lamb is well enough in a day or two to go back to its mother. Any animal that he works with usually survives. He has a way about him to help keep things alive.

My granddad studies his sheep and props himself against a gate and stands and watches them for the longest time. He usually knows which ewes are about to lamb, and he can tell which ewes are not giving enough milk and which little ones are not getting enough. I don't know how he knows so much about them. It must be just because he takes a special interest like maybe God asked him to.

Crit and Sollie were about finished milking when we got to the dairy barn, so my granddad went on to the house to clean up and settle in. I helped rinse out the milk strainer and buckets in the milk house while talking with Crit and Sollie. I like talking with them, because they treat me like I'm almost grown up, and they like for me to be around and help them with the work. We have fun when we're working together and can talk. It isn't like mowing hay all day by yourself out on a hill with only the horses and you and the hot sun. They have many stories to tell, and know I like to hear them. They don't have much in the way of possessions. Their families are about their only possessions, so they don't have to worry about a lot of other things. Each day's work provides what they need. We are all happy most of the time, and near quitting time is the best part of each day. It had been dark for nearly two hours. The lanterns gave off just enough light to make all around us seem unreal. The barn seemed so big, almost endless as it stretched up into the night. Inside, the shadows from the cows made them appear as if they were some kind of monsters as their mouths slowly chomped on the mounds of hay in the feed trough. With their stomachs getting full and the relief of their empty bags, they became content and seemed to understand that we would leave them until the early morning. It's a good feeling and calming to know you've protected and taken care of them.

Outside, the sleet had turned to snow. Large flakes were falling, and when the lantern light seemed to send a golden spark to the center of each snowflake, they became like daisies waving in a summer field. But we'd soon be by warming fires and quietly listening to the stories the flames would tell. The barn would be warmer too when the door was closed against the stormy night.

It happened a year ago, which was in January of 1946. That year was a wonderful year, because the war had ended a few months before. I was seven when the war broke out in 1941 and didn't understand why people wanted to kill other people. I'll be 13 in July, but still don't understand why people want to kill other people, but I guess we had a good reason to try and kill Japs and Germans back then. I did understand that we had to do our part at home. We gathered up scrap metal to make tanks and guns, and did without many things so our country could give our soldiers all they needed. I proudly wore a sweatshirt to school that had "Remember Pearl Harbor" on the front. On the radio, President Franklin Roosevelt kept reminding my granddad that we would win the war and our soldier boys would come home. He was partly right. We won the war, but not all came home.

Four of my uncles made it back from the war, and had to get reacquainted again with their wives, families and new jobs. Two of my older second cousins did not come home. One was shot down in a plane over Germany, and the other was shot down over the Pacific and was never found. I remember my mother bursting into tears when hearing that one of her closest cousins was missing in action. I had never seen my mother cry before. The demands of life on the farm are many and never ending, and crying is a sign of weakness.

It's all right to cry, though, when a family member dies or goes off to war, because the family is the most important part of life. We have many relatives and lots of them come for a visit. My great aunt Lina comes and stays with us for weeks at a time. My great Granddad Frank Conrad used to visit for a few days, and all of our attention was directed toward him. Aunts, uncles, and cousins come for Sunday dinners. When the preacher comes for Sunday dinner, we have to eat in the dining room, and I have to keep my church clothes on, which makes me feel kind of stiff and tight. At first, I thought we would have to talk mostly about Jesus, but after a few pieces of fried chicken, the preacher usually seems to loosen up and we even laugh at times if the talk is about real life.

It is always a treat to have relatives visit our place, and older people are special in a way. We listen to them, because they tell us about how they raised their families and about the things they did in their lives. After milking and supper, we sit on the front porch during the summer, or by the big kitchen fireplace in the winter and listen to their stories. Young people are supposed to listen so they can learn something.

The war was hard for everybody. Shoes, gasoline, and many food items were rationed. We only bought what we had to have. In springtime, many children and younger people began going barefoot, in order to save shoe leather. The poorer ones shed their shoes in very early spring before the frosts gave way to the warmer coats of dew. Travel to town occurred only when necessary. We didn't have a car most of those years during the war, and relatives or neighbors took us to town, 11 miles away, when we had to go. Sometimes, my mother, younger sister and I hitched a ride with Pete, our milk truck driver, who picked up the ten-gallon cans of milk each morning at our farm. We rode with him to town and stayed a day or two with my aunt. In town, we could get candy bars, soft drinks, chewing gum, light bread, and sometimes we went to the picture show.

During the war, many of the clothes that we needed were ordered from the Sears, Roebuck catalogue. When the big package came, it was always exciting to open it and see a new coat or sweater for winter. Any package in the mail was like a Christmas morning. One day, I went to the mailbox, and a package addressed to me was hanging from the mailbox post. I had never received a package before, and I hurriedly took it to the house. One of my uncles, who was in the Army, had sent me a baseball glove and ball. It was the best gift I had ever received, and made me so happy. I cherish the glove, and hold it on cold winter nights and pound the ball into the pocket to keep it loosened up. On Sunday afternoons during the summer, Jimmy and Henry, who live on neighboring farms, come to our barn lot, and we play flies and grounders. On other days when work is done or on rainy days when we have to come in from a field, I

9

make up my own games. I bounce my ball off the side of the milk house and pretend that I'm the Cincinnati Reds first baseman scooping up a hot grounder. I also throw it high up on the barn roof, let it roll back off, and pretend that I've made a game-saving catch.

I never have much time for ball games of any sort. Time is spent working, and work is never finished. My granddad is known as a hard worker, and through years of struggling, was able to save enough to make a down payment on the farm. He taught me how to work, and I know I have to work along with him every day. Sundays are the Sabbath days, and rest days as the Bible says, but even on those days, the milking and feeding have to be done. There are many kinds of work on the farm that the very young can do. He's taught me that those who work the hardest are the ones who get ahead in life.

When in school, I work before and after every school day. After school, eggs have to be gathered, corn shelled and fed to the hens, stove wood split and carried in from the wood shed, and the milk cows brought in from the pasture field. During certain seasons, I have to gather apples, pears, walnuts and hickory nuts. I have a couple of hours for this work, and then I help with the milking and feeding at the end of the day. Before the school bus comes in the mornings, I usually have to get the workhorses from the field and harness them so they are ready for work after milking. Each morning, I also bring Lady from the field, saddle her, and rein her to the gate behind the house, so my granddad can ride out over the farm and check on the fences, crops, cattle, and sheep.

Lady is his riding mare and is a part of him, because he spends most of every day with her. She is a sleek sorrel mare with a white splotch on her forehead. She is smaller than the workhorses, and is never harnessed for work. He always rides her from hollow to hollow, ridge to ridge and field to field in a run-and-walk gait. This gait is a smooth and easy flowing movement, and is about three times as fast as a regular walk. Much of his time is spent astride her back, and the two of them can cover a lot of ground during a day together. She seems to understand what he wants her to do, and is soon in the run-and-walk gait whenever he mounts her. If they are moving sheep to another field, she goes toward a stray or one that is lingering behind the flock without a command from him. Lady and my granddad understand how to work together, and she seems to know what he wants.

In a way, though, all we do seems important, because everything on our farm — gardens, crops, hayfields, pastures, hills, woods, creeks, barns and animals — is such a part of our life. When about all you do is try to keep everything on the farm the way it should be, you can't overlook anything. It's like when Mom cooks a big Sunday dinner for a lot of uncles, aunts and cousins when they come to visit in the summer. She always tries to make the big table on the back porch look good and nice for them. She makes it all come together somehow, and it would worry her if she overlooked anything.

The fried spring chicken has to have white gravy with it to cover the hot biscuits. Yellow churned butter coats the new potatoes and the roasted ears of corn. The green beans are set next to a bowl of sliced onions and cucumbers swimming in sugar water and vinegar. She places sliced red and yellow tomatoes alongside a plate of green peppers. Glasses of white milk or deep brown tea are put beside each plate. Before the blessing, Mom takes a big dark-red berry cobbler from the oven so it will cool enough to be just right at the end of dinner. I guess that's what my granddad does with the farm. He somehow makes it all come together at the end of each day as best he can.

When my granddad and I went after the sheep that cold day, it was late and near milking time. I don't actually remember when I first began milking. I help milk now some, but there's so much else to do during that time. In the summer, the cows have to be brought in from the pasture. During a dry summer, the cows are often driven to a back pasture in the mornings, and bringing them to the barn in the evening might take nearly an hour. After my granddad, Crit and Sollie fill the buckets with the warm foamy milk, I take the full buckets to the milk house and empty them into a strainer over a ten-gallon can.

In summer, the milk can is placed into a vat of cool water pumped from the milk house cistern, and I stir each can of milk long enough for the surrounding water to cool it. This prevents the fresh, warm milk from spoiling before Pete picks it up early the next morning in his big International truck and takes it to Cincinnati.

In the winter, I have to throw hay down from the loft and silage from the silo. When finished with a big mound of each, I take a large scoop shovel of the moist silage and place it in front of each stanchion where the 20 cows are standing. I pour a half-gallon of crushed corn on top of the silage, and the cows begin their meal with a dessert. The sweet smell of the silage topped off with the golden nuggets of crushed corn is a delight for the hungry cows. I like to watch them eat. It gives satisfaction to watch any animal eat. It makes me feel important to feed them.

It's usually near dusk during the gray winter days when it is time for milking. The cows gather near the cow-lot gate. The bags of the big black and white Holsteins are full and waiting for relief. Two of our cows are golden-yellow and white Guernseys, and two are solid-brown Jerseys. I like the little Jerseys the best, because they're so gentle and delicate. Sometimes the bigger Holsteins try to push them around, so I try to help protect the smaller ones. The Holsteins give most of the milk, which is sold by the pound and also based on the butterfat content. The Guernseys and Jerseys give less milk, but it is very high in butterfat and is mixed in with the Holsteins milk. When the milk parlor door is opened, the cows crowd around the cow-lot gate, and when it is opened, the Holsteins lead the rush to the barn. Since pastures are nearly barren during the winter, they get little to eat during the day. It doesn't take them long to eat their mound of silage and crushed corn, and they lick every scrap from the trough in front of their stanchion.

When Crit and Sollie begin milking it doesn't take long for them to fill a bucket. In the summer, I like to watch Crit's arms while he milks, and my how he can make the milk foam. His big strong arms move up and down ever so slightly, but the veins, tendons and muscles ripple across his arms, while the sweat drips and the milk rises quickly up to the rim of the bucket. He has a way about him that is smooth, and the cats come to the back of the cow he is milking, and he squirts streams of warm milk ever so gently into their mouths.

When the feed troughs in front of the cows are licked clean of the silage, I fork hay that I threw down from the loft into the troughs. Some years, we have a good alfalfa crop, and this is the best hay, but my granddad always wants to make sure he has enough alfalfa for the sheep. If it has been a good growing year, then the cows get a lot of alfalfa. The large hayloft over the dairy barn is filled with layers of timothy hay mixed with red clover, sweet clover or white clover and a section for the alfalfa. In dry years, we have to use weedy fields for hay.

It is important to have good clover hay that's high in nutrients, because good hay produces more milk. My granddad sort of learned this on his own, but when he began talking to the county agriculture agent, he learned many other things about what smart college men and experts were telling any farmers who would listen. He likes the county agent, and tries to do many of the things that the county agent tells him. The county agent knows a lot about what they call scientific farming. He learned this from the University of Kentucky experimental farm. My granddad understands the old ways of farming are not always the best way. He only had a fourth-grade education, but he is smart in many other ways.

When I fork the hay into the trough, the cows begin their slow chewing of the hay, and with their bags drained, they too seem at peace with the approaching night. They like their home in the barn. It becomes warmer throughout the night as their body heat fills the space under the full hayloft above them. The barn is their shield and comfort against the cold night winds.

The barn is another home for us in a way. It's a place for children to play and men to work. It's a place where we spend a lot of time. It's a place for the cows, horses, sheep, sparrows, barn martins and cats. It's a place for man and animals to get protection from rain and storms and cold. It's a place to fix harness, repair wagons and plows, and a place in summer to fill with hay, silage and corn. It's a place to be cleaned of manure and chaff. It's a warm place in winter and a cool place in summer. It's a place to shear sheep, doctor calves and curry horses. It's a place to rest from work, and sit on a milk stool, whittle, talk or watch the barn martins scurry in and out. The barn has its own sights, sounds and scents. The scents are very noticeable. The air in the barn lot is fresh and clean, but near the barn door, a musty world of scent cuts through any air. The barn stands sturdy and strong, but each season of the year has its time where the air inside tells a different story. It's like in the house where the smell of fried chicken simmers in the skillet in summer, but in winter the sausage gives off its strong and warming scent when we come in from the cold.

The smells from the barn in summer are different with the musty smoldering of the new hay in the loft, and the cow hoofs caked with

13

blue mud from watering at the pond before milking time. The only smell I do not like is in early spring, when wild onions take growth before the grass begins to green, and the cows, wanting fresh sprigs, eat the wild onion shoots. Sometimes the milk has a bitter onion taste, and the city dairy rejects the tainted milk. The urine and manure in the pit behind the cows always has a bitter scent, but we're used to it and it doesn't bother us. When the warm milk begins to flow, its sweetness seems to overrule the other smells. The steam from the horses, wet with a summer's rain and unharnessed in their stalls with clover and corn grains in their bin, combine to make their scent strong and bold. The winter smells are trapped, because the doors stay closed against the cold. Silage has the sweetest smell. Its moist and blended slivers of stalks and leaves and ears from a stand of corn are like sweet kraut, apples and pure spices all in one.

At the end of a winter day, the cats go to the loft for the night to sleep in the warm hay. After chewing their mound of hay, the cows lie down on the bedding of chaff and straw. When the barn doors are closed and latched, all is soon quiet in the barn, and the night becomes still. After the milk buckets and strainer are washed at the milk house, the day's work is done. Crit and Sollie each fill a gallon bucket of fresh milk to take to their families. I like to follow them down the lane and watch them go over the hill with their lantern and buckets of milk. When snow is on the ground, the light from the lanterns makes the snow appear as if it has been sown with bright diamond seeds.

Mom has supper ready soon after we come in from milking. It's usually something like fried cured sausage, milk gravy, a quart jar of green beans seasoned with cured jowl bacon, fried potatoes, pickled beets, biscuits, yellow churned butter, sorghum molasses, berry jam, and fresh milk. All of the food comes from the earth on our farm. Coffee, sugar, salt and baking powder are about the only food we need to buy at a store.

After coming in from the barn, my granddad and I hang our winter coats over the stacked firewood on the back porch, and put our dirty boots near the kitchen door. Before we got the kitchen stove, I used to like standing by the big fireplace in the kitchen and watch my shadow against the cold wall across the room. It made me look so tall. And before we got electricity, the kerosene lamp on the table gave off a flickering soft light making the room seem like there were ghosts there.

When the hot biscuits are removed from the oven of the cook stove, supper is ready. During the war, my granddad tried to make it in for supper in time to listen to Lowell Thomas on our radio. He wanted to hear about the war. Although he never said much about it, I know he was worried, with his only son and son-in-law off to the war. My granddad seldom talks about how he feels about serious things, but I can tell by the way he acts. He gazes away when he is worried, and seems to be thinking in a deep sort of way. I don't like to see him worried. When Lowell Thomas came on the radio, we had to be quiet and listen. My granddad would not say anything while he ate and listened to reports about the war. If the report was good, my granddad would perk up. If Lowell Thomas told us that President Roosevelt had said something encouraging, my granddad would sometimes smile. He called President Roosevelt, "the old man," and put his faith in him and felt he knew what he was doing and could lead us to peace.

# CHAPTER TWO

## THE LAY OF OUR LAND

Our farm is in Pendleton County, Kentucky, and it's a pretty place. It's mostly hills and ridges that kind of roll down into creeks and hollows. Out the back door of our house, you can see way down over the hills and valleys far away. I never feel closed up where we live. It's not like the towns and cities, where people are packed together. I do like going to town whenever I can, and get to go to Cincinnati, Ohio once or twice a year. We live about halfway between Lexington, Kentucky and Cincinnati, Ohio, which is about 45 miles north, and a very big city. It's really exciting to see the tall buildings and big stores. The people there are dressed so nice, and many of them have good Sunday-like clothes on every day. They talk kind of funny, though, and use bigger words than we do. We used to go to the Cincinnati Zoo every year, because the milk company where we ship our milk, would send us tickets. The past couple of years, one of my uncles has taken me to see the Cincinnati Reds play a baseball game, and that is one of the best things I've ever done in my life. My real dad, who lives in Lexington, took me to one of their games once, and we ate hot dogs and cold soft drinks and had a big bag of peanuts. It was wonderful. The grass on the field there is almost a perfect green, and when the big lights shine down on the pretty white and red uniforms when they run out on the field, it's almost like I'm in a dream.

Falmouth is the county seat of our county, and we live 11 miles from there. Some of my relatives live in town, and we usually get to visit them every couple of weeks. It's not a very big town, but I like going there, because of the stores and the picture show and all the people who live there. They get to see each other nearly every day. I think life is much easier for town people. The boys that I know there don't have to work very much, and some of them don't work any. They get to play ball everyday with each other and go to the store everyday, and they sure get a lot more soft drinks and candy bars than I do. And they get to talk to each other all the time. Being alone so much, I sometimes have to just talk to myself. I don't usually talk out loud, but talk in a thinking way. I think about myself a lot and wish that I didn't have to be responsible for so many things. Most of the town boys live in houses that have a coal furnace in the basement, and they don't even have to carry in wood.

It's funny that we live at both Short Creek and at Goforth. The community was called Short Creek, because the Baptist church was first built down on Short Creek, which runs along the back of our farm. When the store was built years ago, and a post office was put there, there was already a Short Creek post office in Kentucky. They had to give it a different name, so somebody came up with the name of Goforth. Our farm is about two miles from the Goforth School, and a mile and a half from the Short Creek Baptist Church and Elmer and May Perry's big country store. You can get about anything you need at Elmer's store. He has tin cans of food, a candy case, an ice box with soft drinks, flour, sugar, coffee, oatmeal, shoes, thread, matches, milk buckets, hoe handles and gas for cars. We don't buy too much from Elmer, but Crit and Sollie do. They usually take a big burlap sack with them and walk to Elmer's after milking on Saturday night, and buy what they need for their families for the coming week or until the huckster truck comes on Wednesdays. I like to walk to the store with them, because the week's work is done and it's a good feeling. We can talk and tell stories and laugh on the way. I can take a dime and get me a soft drink and a candy bar, which tastes mighty good, especially if it is the first one of the week.

Goforth School is my school. It is a nice brick building that was built during the Depression by the WPA, which was started by the government and President Roosevelt. The WPA put people to work during the depression, because there were so many people who didn't have jobs. The new building took the place of a wooden three-room building. We have four teachers, and each teacher teaches two grades. I'm in the seventh grade, and the way it works is that the teacher gives out spelling words to us while the eighth grade is studying their spelling words. Then she gives out the eighth grade spelling words. Reading and arithmetic work the same way. Of course, I hear her give out words to the eighth grade and I can learn some of their words along with my own. I'll already know most of the eighth grade words when I get there next year.

I can't wait to get to Morgan High School after I finish Goforth next year. It's a big school with over 100 students in the high school part. It's located right on the bank of the South Licking River. It's about eight miles from our house, and the way to get there is over a rough gravel road, but I won't mind because in high school, the boys are almost like men. Some of them drive their own cars and take girls to the picture show on Saturday nights. Kenny Willis, who lives down the road past Elmer's store and goes to our church, is a junior at Morgan. He is the brother of Jimmy Willis, who is my good friend, and Jimmy rides his bicycle up to our place on Sunday afternoons and we play ball and go to the store. We used to play mostly in the barn, but now we play either baseball or basketball since we are older. Anyway, Kenny has a 1940 Chevy coupe, and he's pretty wild and drinks beer. I'm not interested in drinking beer when I get in high school, because all I want to do is play on the Morgan Raiders basketball team.

The town of Morgan has about ten houses, two stores, a post office, and a church and it used to have a bank and a doctor's office. The railroad goes right through the middle of it. The best thing about Morgan High School is the gym. One time we boys at Goforth got to go there and shoot basketball in the gym. It was wonderful. The floor is shiny, and it sure beats our court outside on the dirt and rocks at Goforth. The Morgan Raiders wear gold uniforms with blue numbers, and I can't wait to wear one of them and play in a real game in a real gym. I hope I'm good enough to make the team my freshman year and I think I am. I shoot goals out on the barn whenever I can, and can make many of my shots. I am left-handed, and other boys can't get used to shots from my left hand, but I can hit the basket pretty well. My granddad says though that I'm too awkward in driving a nail or anything else in using a tool on the farm.

We study a lot of subjects, but history is probably my favorite, especially the presidents. My granddad talks about Franklin Roosevelt a lot whenever he's around other men. He thinks President Roosevelt led us out of the Depression and saved us from the Japs and Hitler. He also thinks Franklin Roosevelt saved him his farm. I think he also likes Harry Truman, from what he says, but not as much as President Roosevelt. I don't know much about the Depression, because I was just a baby when it happened. But it must have been pretty rough.

When my granddad talks about the Depression, he gets real serious and acts like he's almost scared. I said almost, because he never acts like he's scared of anything. They didn't have much back then, but I certainly remember when most everything was rationed during the war, and I learned that you just couldn't have very much of anything. There was no use wanting something when you knew you couldn't get it, so you didn't waste time wanting. During the war, we had to help out any way we could, and we gathered up all the scrap metal we could find like old tools and old mowing machines and broken plows. The metal was all sent away to make things for the war. The government gave us ration stamps, because many things were very scarce. You needed a ration stamp to buy a pair of shoes, so my feet got tough from going barefoot so much in order to save on shoes. You also had to have a ration stamp to buy gasoline, and you couldn't drive more than 35 miles per hour so as to save gas for jeeps, tanks and bombers. We didn't have a car during most of the war, because they were scarce. When the old ones broke down, you couldn't get parts or a new one, because they were not making cars, but only machines and things for the war. We had to save on everything. Sugar was real scarce, and we got used to either eating without it or using honey and sorghum for sweetening. When the war was over, I remember how happy everybody was, mainly because our fighting boys were coming home. Everything is much better now, but we are still worried some, because Korea and Russia may want to make the world into Communism. I don't worry too much about going into the army and fighting, since I'm still pretty young, but I know that one day I'll probably have to go. Some people say that we may not have to fight with guns as much since we now have the atomic bomb, which beat the Japs real quick toward the end.

I like school and learning. It may be because my granddad missed out, and he can now see that schooling might help you to get a sit-down job in the future so you don't have to work so hard. My mom graduated from high school, as did most of my uncles and aunts. But many people out in the country don't see a need for too much book learning. You can't study how to plow ground from a book. But my granddad knows he missed out, and he made sure my mom and his other two kids graduated from high school. She went to Goforth when it was a high school. It was a three-room building that sat on a ridge just across the hollow from our church. There were five in her class, but the building is no longer there, and only two concrete steps remain, and sit out there lonely-like in a field. When they started running school buses a few years back, those who wanted to go on to high school could go to Morgan High over on the South Licking River where I'll go in a couple of years.

My granddad likes to read, and I think it tells him that he might have made something of himself like a doctor or lawyer or a high-up government person if he only had an education. When he reads, he gets very quiet and serious, and seems to be away from us. It's like he's looking off far away and thinking about something else. It might be like how I feel sometimes, wishing that I were a town boy and that I got to do all they get to do. It's like if you miss out on something, there seems to be an aching that stays with you.

Our mailman gets to our house about the time we start dinner, and as soon as dinner is over, I go to the mailbox and get the paper and any letters. Not too many people in the country take a daily newspaper. We get the Louisville *Courier Journal*, and my granddad knows a lot about what's going on in the world. He likes to read a little of it while we go hitch up the horses and get ready for whatever we have to do during the afternoon. After church on Sundays, he tells the other men about the government and other things, and seems to get a little excited when he's talking about Joseph Stalin of Russia, or other parts of the world.

He doesn't talk too much to Crit and Sollie about news, because they're not real interested and don't understand much about it anyway. In a way, if you don't know much about war and bad things that are always happening, you don't have to worry about them. Crit and Sollie are mostly happy with just doing their work, having enough to feed their families, hunting squirrels and rabbits once in a while, and having plenty of good smoking and chewing. Crit smokes Bull Durham, and Sollie chews Day's Work plug. Good cigarettes like Camels, Lucky Strikes and Chesterfields cost more than roll-your-own Bull Durham or Buffalo, so Crit and most poor people buy the cheaper tobacco in sacks with rolling papers. Most tobacco chewers use a little cut of plug and mix it with home-made twist tobacco. It's much cheaper that way, and every nickel counts.

I've tried smoking and chewing, but if my mom and granddad ever found out, they'd be real mad at me. People say that after working in tobacco so much, the nicotine kind of gets in your blood, and then you crave it, so most farmers either smoke or chew. My granddad used to smoke a pipe, but he's given it up in his older days, and I know he doesn't want me ever smoking, although he's never exactly said it. Most of the older boys smoke, and some eighth graders do. When he was in the eighth grade, Stanley Barnes used to put a chew in his mouth during recess. He used his ink bottle to spit in during lessons, and then he'd put it in his pocket and empty it during noon or the next recess. The teacher never caught him, because he was so good at holding in the spit when he had to. He never went on to high school, and I think it was because he knew it would be harder to chew there in the rooms.

Out in the country and away from towns, every little area about four or five miles apart has a store, a church and maybe a school and a blacksmith. Bud Klein's store at Locust Grove is about three miles west of us, and he stays open on Sunday, because he's not religious. He's known to drink beer and whiskey and is kind of rough, and my mother doesn't want me going there too much. Elmer's store is not open on Sundays, so Jimmy and Henry and I ride our bicycles to Bud's on some Sunday afternoons after playing ball, and get big Pepsis out of his ice-box, and the cold bottle almost makes your hand ache. In the summer, Henry Cooper also lives with his granddad and grandmother on the farm next to ours. He is two years older than me and is my best friend. When we were little boys, we would go down into the woods back of their house and build cabins out of tree branches or saplings. Henry was always scared to take his granddad's hatchet, but sometimes he would try to sneak it out. Henry was smart and was always telling me what he knew from reading about things in books. And he could imagine many things about forts and huts that would protect us from Indians or robbers. When we went to the woods, he always had plans, and most of them worked out. Now that we're older, we mostly play ball and talk about high school and things in the future.

If it is hard to get to a store, you can always depend on Charlie Wright's huckster truck. It's a big truck with wooden sides and shelves all along the inside from top to bottom. He comes along about milking time every Wednesday. He pulls up in front of the barn and blows his horn, and you can get what groceries you want and talk with him for a while. He never seems in a hurry about anything, and it must be awfully late at night when he finally makes it back to town. Charlie usually has enough groceries to sell that you could make it to the next week. Some of the older people and those without cars rely on Charlie to bring them what they need. If they need something he doesn't have, he will bring it to them next week. He usually has a big barrel with salty brine fish inside, and people liked to have fish in the wintertime once in a while. He also carries jowl bacon and cured side meat for people who don't have much meat or have run out. Everybody needs a little meat to cook with soup beans and to make enough grease for gravy. Charlie likes to talk to you, and he asks me about how I'm doing as a basketball player and my future at Morgan High. He lifts my spirits, because he seems really interested in me and how I'm doing. Most of the older people don't say much to you. I don't know, maybe it's because they have too many worries, but when a grown up talks to me about me, it makes me feel like I might be important.

Crit and Sollie buy quite a bit from Charlie since they have several kids each. Many of the tenant farmers and the poorer people never seemed to know how to make ends meet. They don't can much garden food and don't cure much meat to last. They live mainly on dried soup beans, biscuits, cornbread and always milk gravy on everything. They always have plenty of milk from the cows for drinking and making clabber and butter. They have plenty of eggs from the chickens, and in the summer they have tomatoes, green beans, onions, cucumbers, corn and frying chickens. For meat, they fry up rabbits and squirrels, and some will eat a big old groundhog now and then. At the huckster, they'll fill up a burlap sack, sling it over their shoulders and head down the ridge to their homes. If they have a little extra money, they buy a small sack of candy kisses for their kids. Charlie always has plenty of molasses kisses with peanut butter inside on his truck. I'm always glad when Crit and Sollie have enough money left to buy a piece or two for each little kid.

We're better off than the tenant farmers and poor people and usually have a way to get to a store or town for the things we need. And of course, Mom cans nearly everything, and we usually have plenty of beef, lamb, chickens and cured pork to eat. My granddad helps our tenant farmers out with meat and many other things, if he thinks their kids aren't getting enough to eat. Sometimes Mom has me get baking powder or something like that from Charlie, and I usually get two packs of chewing gum each week, which has to last me until the next week when he comes around again.

Most families live on farms that are around 100 acres in size. They can make a living on one that size, although it might not be a very good living. My granddad has always been known as a hard worker and a good farmer and takes pride in doing a good job. A few years ago, he bought an adjoining farm to make ours one of the biggest around with 444 acres in all. It's a hill farm with about a third of it in bushes, thickets and woods and the rest of it cleared for pastures and crops. It takes a lot of work to clear land, but we keep clearing a little each year. The hills are pretty steep, but not so steep they can't be plowed and worked. The ridges along the top of the hills slope down and glide toward little creeks that flow into the beginning of Short Creek at the back of the farm. Small patches of fertile bottom land run alongside some of the creeks.

Many of the poorer farmers still do things the old way and plow and crop the steep hills for corn or tobacco. The government recommends that farmers plow up only the ridges, so that the land won't wash away. We do this, except sometimes we have to plow up a whole hillside in order to grow enough corn to fill our big silo. We grow hay on many of the hillsides and use the other ones for pasture.

Our house and main buildings are on the main road, which is a very winding black-topped road that runs from Falmouth to Williamstown. Our house is a big two-story frame house that my great-grandfather built after he got out of the Civil War. We use the fireplaces to heat it in the cool part of fall and spring, but use wood stoves during the main part of winter. The fireplace in the kitchen is a big one and it can take a log about the size of two-bushel baskets put together. We've got plenty of water, with one cistern on one side of the house and one on the other. In the summer at dinner time, I pump water into a wash tub out of the cistern by the smoke house. The sun heats it up in the afternoon, and when I get in from milking at night, I've got a tub of warm water for a bath at the smokehouse. One of the cisterns has a pipe running to it, and we use a hand pump to pump water into the kitchen sink.

Fairly close to our house are the outhouse, the smoke house, the wood house and the chicken house. A little ways away is the dairy barn with a tall silo, the corncrib, a tool shed and the milk house. The dairy barn has 20 stanchions for the milk cows, seven other stalls for horses, sheep or dry cows and a room for harness and saddles. This big barn has a hay loft, which holds maybe forty wagon loads or more of hay. The tile silo over 60 feet tall stands next to the barn, and when I throw down the silage, it lands in a big pile right next to the feeding trough for the milk cows. Sweet moist silage smells so good, and the cows like it like I like ice cream. Each cow gets a big scoop-shovel full twice a day, and seeing them go after it on a cold winter day gives you satisfaction. You never have to drive the cows in from the cow-lot when they smell the silage. They run in to get to it.

Next to the dairy barn is a good-size pond for watering, and beyond it is the tobacco barn with the stripping room. All these buildings around the house are important, and we spend a lot of time working in and around them. Of course, I used to play out in the barns. You can play hide-and-go-seek all around the mangers and up in the hayloft, slide down the hay mounds in the loft, climb up in the railings where we hang tobacco in the tobacco barn and have corncob fights in the horse stalls. There are many things you can do in the way of playing on a farm. We'd dig out hollers and build cave houses and sometimes wander back to the creeks and make little dams out of rocks and mud. There were many things you could dream up and pretend to be doing, like being Tarzan on a grapevine down in the woods, or actually get the horses, and ride out fast to the range to escape the outlaws. Now that I'm older, it's mostly baseball and basketball.

A farmer seems to have two homes, because he spends about as much time at the barn as he does at the house. When coming in out of the fields to the barn it's restful in a way, because it's the time when you have about finished the day's work. Although the milking has to be done, you can sit on the milk stool while doing it, and this is an easier job than forking hay, plowing corn, hauling rock and most other jobs out in the field. In the summer, it gives satisfaction to come in and take the harness off the sweaty, tired horses and turn them out to pasture. You know they appreciate it, because of the way the younger ones run and romp to the pasture gate behind the corncrib. In the winter, it gives satisfaction to know that the barn has provided a warm place for so many creatures. The sounds and smells of a barn become as much of your nature as listening to the kettle boil on the stove and smelling the sausage frying in the skillet. It just seems to be a place where you feel like you do at the house, where you feel good and peaceful and restful like. I guess you could say that home even includes the land and everything that goes with it. It seems like you can't separate any of it. It either all becomes a part of you, or nothing does.

The lay of our land is hard to explain unless you can see it. It's mostly hills with long ridges running across the tops and tapering off down into gullies and small creeks. There are two main ridges extending out from our house. One goes down to where our two tenant houses are, the other main ridge goes off toward the west, and we call it the Joe Hand place. The Joe Hand place is very interesting to me, because he was a freed slave. Where his house used to stand there is still a big hole in the ground where he had his cellar. His well still has water in it, and a pear tree still stands nearby. It has good sweet pears every couple of years, and whenever I pick and eat one, I wonder what it was like when those freed slaves ate pears from this old tree.

I don't know much about the slaves or Negroes, because I seldom ever see a Negro. I do know that Abraham Lincoln freed the slaves during the Civil War, and that my granddad's dad was in the Union Army. Mrs. Poore, who lives up the road and is over 90, remembers when she was a little girl watching Rebel soldiers marching down the road. We study wars in history and it is interesting when you think that Rebel soldiers marched down the road in front of your house.

There is something about the Joe Hand place that I like, and it's kind of a mystery as to why I like it. There is a grove of walnut trees above where his house was, and our sheep like to gather there in the shade during the hot days. It is a real pretty place, and when I have to go drive them up, I always think and wonder what it was like when a freed slave first had a place of his own.

With a big farm, it's probably close to a mile and a half from our house to the back part of it, where we have a few little creek bottoms running alongside the beginning of Short Creek. The two tenant houses where Crit and Sollie and their families live are back on the main ridge about halfway to the end of our place. Crit and his four kids and wife live in the first house, which has three rooms. Sollie, his wife and five kids live in the next one, and it has four rooms. They each have an outhouse, a chicken house and a cistern for drinking. Crit's family also uses the spring down in the hollow in front of his house, because the water is sweeter and cooler.

We've had many different tenant farmers through the years. Many of them are mountaineers and came north because they got tired of working the coal mines. Some of them were very good workers and tried to get ahead. They all had to work, because if they didn't, my granddad wouldn't put up with them. Whenever my granddad said, "he's a good worker," you knew he liked the tenant. According to him, a good worker will go ahead and keep at it, and not stop at the end of every row, if he's chopping out tobacco, and roll a cigarette.

The way it works is that a tenant farmer agrees to work for you during a crop year. He raises a crop of tobacco of his own, but gives half of it to the owner when it is sold. He also agrees to help milk the cows for a percentage of the milk sales. When he is not working in his own crop, he works for my granddad for three dollars a day, and he has to work every day except Sundays. There is always fence to build or fix, wood to cut, weed fields to mow, and other work that is never finished. So at the end of a week, a tenant might have made around nine dollars for groceries for his family of six or seven or more. Of course, when the tobacco sells at the end of the year, he can buy shoes and clothes for the kids.

Most of the tenant farmers can't read or figure. Some can read and figure a little, but there isn't much need to, because they trust my granddad to do them right. When he is ready to pay them at the end of a week or month, he takes his pencil, tears off a piece of paper sack, and shows them how he figured the money. Most of the time, I can see they aren't following him, and they just take what he gives them. He does them right though, because he is known to do right. It sure keeps the trouble down.

As I said, we've had several tenant families come and go during the years. Sometimes they get restless and move on and try to get a regular job on the road or the railroad. A couple of years ago, we had Isaac Carter and his family. He had eight kids and was pretty rough and not very smart. He seemed like he was kind of bewildered by it all, trying to feed 10 people. During one spell, he had a brother, his wife and two kids move in with him, and there were 14 people living in his small four-room tenant house.

His oldest girl, Lucy, was in the eighth grade at the time, and she was the only one of them who liked to go to school. My granddad would explain to her how the money came out at the end of a pay period, because Isaac couldn't understand much of anything. Isaac's family was different than most of the tenant families, because the whole family would go to the field. Most of the tenant's wives stay at the house and cook and take care of the little ones. But Isaac's wife Elsie liked working in the field better than staying in the house. When they lived on our place, she once had a new baby and a week later she was working out in the hay field. She would put the baby in a little box under a shade tree and have one of her younger daughters watch it. When it would start to cry, Elsie would go and sit down under the shade tree and let it nurse. One thing about Isaac's family was that the whole family would rather be in the fields than in the house.

In bad weather, it's pretty hard for the tenant kids to walk up to our house to catch the school bus. So they don't go too often, and most of them really don't like school. If a kid doesn't like school, the dad doesn't make them go. It is also hard to keep them in good shoes and coats, and it is hard to send anything for them to eat at lunch. Most of the poor people don't see how school can help you all that much. You make a living by working, and forking hay, hoeing corn and cutting tobacco, which doesn't take reading.

I played and, as I got older, worked with the tenant farmers and their kids every day. I don't think we are better than they are, but I don't know for sure. My granddad and mom always treat them good, but we never invite them in our house for dinner or things like that. They can come in our house, but don't come in very often. It is understood that way. We can go in their house, but don't go very often, because there is no need to. It's something like city and town people in a way. Some people seem to be higher up. City people don't wear torn-up, dirty clothes that farmers have to wear. And they all go to school every day, and many of them go right on through high school.

The town people talk more about news and things going on in the world. And most town people take a newspaper and magazines and actually talk about what's in them. People on the farm talk more about

27

the crops and the rain and things in nature. Crit and Sollie talk about how their old dog treed a coon last night, or about when pokeberry leaves might be ready for a mess of greens. You never hear town people talk like they do. It seems like I have to learn to talk two ways. I talk one way to the poor people and then try to talk better to people with education. I try to be careful when the preacher comes or when I'm at school with the teachers or go to town. It's hard to talk two ways, because neither one of them seems natural to me.

Being with the tenants and their kids every day, I don't want to act like I'm better or talk like I know a lot more than they do. So I talk according to the way they talk. But I also know that when I go to high school and maybe even to college, I will have to quit talking like them. In a way, though, they just take every day as it comes. If you don't have to look ahead, then you don't have to worry too much, and you don't have to keep learning new things to get ahead. It is like they think they'll never get much improvement, so just do the work, and rest up at night and listen to the Renfro Valley Barn Dance and the Grand Ole Opry and Little Jimmy Dickens on the battery radio. About all they have or seem to need is a few chairs, benches, beds, a kitchen table and a cook stove. The battery radio and getting to the store or the huckster truck once a week is about all the entertainment they ever have except what entertainment they do for themselves. Whenever they go to town and maybe see a picture show it is a happy time for them. They get to go maybe two or three times a year.

My granddad used to let Isaac drive our car to Elmer's store on Saturday after milking, because he had to buy a lot of flour and cornmeal and things for his eight kids. I'd ride along with them some, and on the way, Isaac would always say, "Can't wait to get a good cold Pepsi." It would be his only cold drink of anything for the week, and when we got there, he would get one first and sit down on the front porch in the cool of the evening and hold it and look at it and then almost hesitate to drink it. You could see how good it made him feel by the way he looked. It makes me feel good to see him or anyone else enjoy a little something once in a while. It makes a Pepsi even taste better to me knowing that someone else likes it so. I guess you can get attached to about anybody in a way, when you watch them and kind of feel sorry for them. When you see them do something as little as staring at a cold drink with a peaceful kind of look, it makes you feel closer to them.

I was explaining how our farm is laid out, but got into everything else. Of course, the barns and the buildings are important, but each hill and ridge and wood and creek is as of much importance as anything else. Each field, each tree, each blackberry patch and each part of the land has its own meaning. The surface of the land might change with a new crop or a new growth of briars and bushes, but it all stays the same. The heat of the sun might burn it, and the freeze might stun it, but the land remains firm and strong. Walking over a hill or down a lane or a cow path or through a woods, you know each part, and it is as familiar as your bed at night.

You know each foot of the land like you know the cupboard in the kitchen. You know where the quail roost, where the squirrels scamper and where the foxes roam. You know the best ground for corn, the best creek flats for tobacco plant beds and the best groves for hickory nuts. You live with the land, walk it, plow it, mow it and can sit down on a rock and listen to its life. It has a life of its own, because it never sleeps and never dies. It's like it's always making a meal for you. After a long morning of forking hay in the hot sun, you can't really explain how good it feels to wash up and then sit on the cool back porch waiting for the hot bowls to come. The taste of the corn and the beans and the tomatoes and the meat and the milk and the biscuits and a sweet cobbler at the end gives you the strength to go on. Each day, the land paints a picture for you, but the picture is never the same as the colors change with the sun and the clouds and the seasons. It changes like it's a different meal, but it doesn't change. I can't explain the land, can't explain how it lays or how it is. You have to live on it to understand.

I can't explain how I really feel about it. As you can probably tell, I have mixed feelings when I think about how hard farm life can be. And yet, I feel so free and easy in a way, whenever I stop for a minute and think of how it has a hold on me.

Maybe it's the way my granddad acts about it. He never really talks about his inside feelings, but when he rides Lady out over the hills every day, and if nothing else, just looks around, I can see he feels importance in what he's doing. Especially when he sits up on her back and his sheep come up to him, I know he has some kind of deep feeling about it all. Maybe the best way is just to tell what happens and my feelings will come out, or not come out.

Everything seems to go round and round. It's like a wagon wheel turning over and over as it goes along. You see people getting older, and I'm getting older, because I think about new things more and more. My granddad is getting older, because he's slowing down from what he used to be. I'm speeding up, and he's slowing down. You see the seasons change and the crops grow and then the harvest, year after year. You see the lambs come and jump and bounce and play, and you see the ewes grow old and die. Every year ends, and then another one starts. Our lambs are born in January, and in December, the ewes are big and fat and ready to bring on a new flock. January is the time when everything starts again on our farm.

# CHAPTER THREE
## BEFORE THE THAW

After the war ended most everything came back to normal. With most of our soldiers getting back home, people were glad to get back to, I guess you'd call it, regular living. You could see everything take on a new light. Work didn't seem to be as much of a drudgery as it was during the war. Soldiers, who came home and went back to farming, were sure glad to work from daylight to dark, and put out more crops than they ever had before.

As we move into February, though, life on our farm goes at a slower pace than any other time during the year. All of the tobacco has been stripped and taken to market. Most all of the lambs are born by this time and are growing and frisky, and it's fun to watch them run out and jump into the air when the barn doors are opened in the morning. There isn't much work that can be done in the fields during these late winter months. Most of the time, snow covers the frozen ground. But when we get a warm spell, the snow melts, and the ground thaws out on top, and the fields and barn lot become very muddy. The cows sink into the earth, and clumps of mud stick to everything.

We still have the feeding and milking morning and evening, and there's always other work to be done. The manure and soggy bedding have to be taken out of the troughs each morning, hay has to be thrown down from the loft and silage from the silo. The barns always need some kind of repair and straightening up.

I like to chop a big hole in the ice in the pond between the dairy barn and the tobacco barn so the animals can get water during frozen times. I like to skate and slide and play on the ice, but my mother is still afraid I'll break through the ice and maybe drown. Whenever the first big freeze comes, I always test out the ice on the pond. One late afternoon a couple of years ago, I broke through the ice up to my waist. I knew my mother would get after me, so rather than going to the house to change pants and shoes, I stayed at the barn during feeding and milking. I thought that by being close to the warm cows maybe my pants would dry and she wouldn't find out. Whenever the muddy times are the worst, we take off our pants on the back porch and put on a cleaner pair before going into the house. When I got to the house, I took off my wet frozen pants and hung them on a nail over the stacked stove wood. She knew that it wasn't a mud time, and went to the porch and felt the wet pants. She got after my granddad as much as she did me for letting me get on the thin ice, but he can't watch me all the time.

Crit and Sollie have more time to hunt during these winter days. Sollie also does some trapping along the creeks and catches foxes, possums, coons, skunks, muskrats, and an occasional mink. He doesn't get too many, but what few pelts he gets, he's able to skin and market, which provides a few extra dollars for his family. Crit likes to hunt without a gun when a big snow is on the ground. He says he can save shotgun shells with a snow on, and this saves him a little money. After a big snow, it is easy to track rabbits or any other varmints and I've gone with him a few times. Hills facing south with briar patches, buck-brush thickets and rock piles are the best places to find rabbits during a heavy snow. Tall dead grass is usually in the center of the patches and thickets, because the cows, horses and sheep can't easily get in there to graze. Rabbits hollow out a little hole in the deep, tall grass and snuggle backwards inside. The hole makes a warm bed.

We start over a hill looking for tracks. If a set of tracks leads to a rock pile, we start moving the rocks. When we spot the rabbit, Crit gets ready to hit it with a rock or stick. If it runs out of its hole and the snow is deep enough so it can't run very fast, Crit usually catches up to it and stuns it with his stick. We do the same thing if we find a rabbit in a briar patch, although it usually runs before Crit can sneak up and stun it. To make the kill, Crit crushes its skull with a rock or with his boot heel. He then takes a piece of twine and ties the rabbit's hind legs to his belt. I've seen him have five rabbits or more tied to his belt. His pant legs down by his knees get coated with blood. He walks home happy, knowing that his family will have fried rabbit, which makes a mighty good feast along with the gravy, biscuits, boiled potatoes and soup beans.

A boy on a farm has to learn to kill. He has to learn how to use a rifle, a shotgun and a knife and sometimes killing has to be done with a rock or club. My granddad even kills chickens by breaking their necks with his hands. I've killed animals, but there is something about it that always makes me feel uneasy and sad. Even when I was little, I watched when it was hog-killing time, and I watched when my granddad went to the chicken house to clean a couple of spring chickens for dinner. Killing animals never seems to bother my granddad and other neighbor men, especially if it is for meat. It is something that is a part of everyday farm life.

We kill rabbits, squirrels, quail, chickens, hogs and beef for food. There is always a good purpose when it means food for a family. We also kill sheep-killing dogs and stray cats and rats, and we kill snakes and groundhogs. Sometimes a dog will get hit and mangled by a car, or another animal will get injured or become so weakly that it's best to go ahead and get them out of their misery. But I always get an uneasy feeling when I kill something. It never seems to bother the older men when they shoot something, but I have a hard time getting used to it. I don't like to see the blood come out. When Crit kills those rabbits out on the cold snow, the blood flows out and runs down into the snow, and it gives me a weak feeling. It feels like maybe some of my blood is left there too. To hear the word "kill" sends a shiver inside me. I know I want to grow up and be a strong man so people will be proud of me, but I'm going to have to start acting like killing animals doesn't bother me. I'll have to get used to having blood on my hands.

I learned to shoot a rifle when I was about seven or eight and first shot a twelve-gauge shotgun a couple of years after that. It almost kicked me down, and Crit, Sollie and my granddad laughed and laughed. I actually had a big bruise on my shoulder, and my mother got kind of mad. She always thought my granddad let me do grown-up things too soon. I know it worried her when I was out with guns or was working with hatchets and axes and corn knives and tobacco spears. She used to be afraid when I climbed all the way up in the silo or climbed to the top rail in the tobacco barn. When I was around six years old, she would worry when I would hitch up our horses, especially the ones that were known to kick and buck. She would worry when seeing me out in the field where the big bull was. She thought all these things were very dangerous for a boy to be around, but I wanted to prove to the men that I was also big in what I could do.

I got a chance to prove myself when a wild dog came after our sheep. It's not that I'm proud of it, but I felt it was my duty, and I know it pleased my granddad. A sheep farmer fears sheep-killing dogs. One early morning, my granddad rushed in and said he heard dogs in the hollow behind our house and thought they might be in the sheep, which were in the field. He hurriedly went to the closet where he kept the guns, and brought out his 12 gauge and 20 gauge shotguns. He gave me the 20 gauge and told me to hurry down the hollow behind our house, and he would go down the ridge. I took the shotgun and could hear yelping as I went. I saw the sheep scurrying up the hill and knew that something bad was happening. When I had gone about a quarter of a mile down the hollow, a rather large, part-breed terrier jumped up out of the creek bed onto the flat. Mixed breeds are the worst. Purebred dogs seldom attack sheep, but when they join the mixed breeds, anything can happen. The spotted-white dog stopped and looked at me with excitement, and stared at me as if to say, "who are you to interrupt my fun?" I lifted the gun, released the safety, and aimed for its head. Pow! The dog dropped. The top part of its head was splattered. I stood there for a minute with many mixed feelings. Some of them were sad ones and some were pride. I had done it. I had helped my granddad, but I had also done something that didn't seem natural. I thought of the sheep and what the dogs could do to them, and I felt good in protecting them. Then I thought of the keen eyes that had stared at me for a moment until I blew them out. It seemed I had to learn that the harmony of nature didn't always work out so that all was well with everything. After standing there for some time, I looked high up to the ridge and could see my granddad with the sheep gathered around him at a fence corner. When I walked up the hill to him, I told him that I had killed the dog. He didn't say much, but I knew he was pleased and maybe proud of me.

Sheep farmers are leery of dogs that roam. Seldom does only one dog attack sheep. But when two or more get together, something vicious returns to their nature. Dogs are strange in a way, because when they start roaming in packs, they will go back to their savage ways and attack innocent animals, which cannot defend themselves. Sheep have no defense whatsoever, and a pack of dogs will attack and mangle or kill sheep for no good reason. They will not eat any of the flesh, but go from one to another and continue ripping the furry wool and skin from a sheep's throat. The worst episode was when a pack of dogs jumped over a gate and got into one of our barns. The sheep were trapped and couldn't scatter out, and the dogs killed 26 of them. My granddad mentions this whenever he's talking to farmers and neighbors about bad times.

My granddad is always a little touchy if he has a flock in a far pasture. He always listens to the sounds of nature, and if he hears barking or yelping dogs in the distance, he becomes alarmed. I've known him to be awakened in the night by barking dogs, and get up to check it out. Most of the time, the dogs are treeing some kind of varmint in a distant hollow, but he goes and finds out what it is. He can usually tell if the pack is in the sheep by the kind of barking they make. It's an excited and alarming sound, and if the sheep are not too far away and the night is still, he can hear the scared and mournful bleating sounds of the sheep.

Good dogs, family dogs, pets, shepherds, bird dogs, feist and foxhounds will for no good reason, join up with ragged curs and strays and form a pack and go after sheep. It is like the story in the Bible of the prodigal son, who went astray. Sometimes, a neighbor's loyal farm dog will be caught in sheep killing. This can cause severe neighborly problems, because you never want to kill a neighbor's dog. But an unwritten law of sheep farmers is that you kill any dog that gets into sheep.

Some of our neighbors keep their dogs tied at night. Clyde Northcutt's farm borders the western part of our farm, and he has a part shepherd that runs loose. One day, my granddad heard the bad sound of dogs over toward the line fence that separates our farm from Clyde's. He took his 12 gauge and hurried to check it out. When he got to the flock, three dogs scampered away, and he thought he recognized one of them as Clyde's dog run up over the ridge towards Clyde' place. He then went to Clyde's barn lot, and saw the dog lying under a shade tree. It appeared to have blood around its mouth. Clyde came out and my granddad told him that his dog had been in our sheep. Clyde got riled up and said he knew his dog was not a sheep-killing dog and that the dog had been in the barn lot all afternoon. Clyde then began acting as if he would fight, but my granddad had a gun.

He had always gotten along with Clyde, although Clyde had many faults. He is a messy farmer, and his gates and fence are always in bad shape and falling down. He spends parts of every day tying up a strand of broken down fence, and Clyde's part of the line fence between our farm and his is often mashed down by a rogue cow or bull. Cattle are always getting from one farm to the other, but my granddad tolerates this most of the time.

Clyde doesn't have many manners. He is a big man with a big gut and he will belch and fart anywhere. His work clothes are usually torn and ripped, and his shoe soles are usually loose and flopping. His big straw hat looks like a hen's nest, but he doesn't seem to mind. He likes to laugh and tell stories and he often tells stories about women and how big their asses or tits are. He is usually dirty and wears overalls for days that might have dried cow manure all over them. He piddles more than he works. He just seems to let life drift by and not let things bother him. His cows are scrawny and scrubby and his horses never have good harness to wear. His barn doors might stay off the hinge for months, and his tobacco crop always needs the weeds chopped out.

His wife Daisy is a church-going woman, and she gets Clyde to go to church with her about once every three or four months. She acts like she has some good upbringing, and neighbors wondered how she ever hooked up with Clyde. Daisy loves to sing hymns, and when we sing at Short Creek Baptist Church, she always sings louder than anybody else does. Daisy adds a little something to the hymns at the end. If we're singing "When the Roll Is Called Up Yonder," and sing "I'll be there," she'll add on real loud at the end an extra, "I'll be there!"

When Clyde comes with her, he acts like he really isn't all that interested, but he has on Sunday clothes and is fairly well cleaned up and shaved. He doesn't look like his natural self. In summer, he sits near one of the open windows at church, and gets fidgety if the preacher gets carried away and preaches too long. Clyde is usually gazing out the church window at Nathan Ballinger's cattle over on the next ridge, and sometimes he swats at flies or sweat bees when they wander into church. Once, when a wasp started circling around his head, he took a cardboard fan donated by the town funeral home and made such a racket that the preacher had to stop until Clyde scared it out the window. Whenever he figures the preacher is about ready for the invitational hymn, Clyde takes his twist of tobacco out of his pocket, tears off a hunk, and pops it into his jaw. That is, if he thinks nobody is looking. One time, somebody got saved and it took up more time than usual. Clyde had a big chew in his mouth, and couldn't wait to spit until the last prayer was over, so he leaned over and spit out the window.

In church, I sometimes watch the people, because the preacher keeps saying the same thing over and over. It's funny when some of the old farmers get real sleepy and their heads bob around and almost fall over.

So, as Clyde and Daisy are our neighbors, we have to stay neighborly with them, and it's important to stay friendly with all your neighbors. My granddad never actually told me this, but I learned it by the way he acts. He is friendly with all our neighbors, although Clyde's neglect of his part of the line fence causes my granddad to get mighty disgusted at times when we have to go run cattle or sheep back and forth. In times of need, we trade work with some of the neighbors. For instance, when it is tobacco setting time, and our plants are big enough to transplant to the field, a neighbor or two comes to help. We then owe them a day's work or so, and go help them when their tobacco plants are ready to plant out in the field.

During these work-trade days, it is always fun to eat dinner in their homes. The women set a big table, which also is part of being neighborly. Most farm dinners are made from the same meat and garden vegetables we have, because most of the food is grown right there on the farms. The women, though, fix different things in a different way. Minnie Wiggins makes a white sauce to cover fresh sliced tomatoes, which my mother never does, and it's really good over them. Nancy Sutton always cooks up apple dishes. Her husband, Benny Sutton, has a lot of apple trees. Nancy fries green apples when they first come on, and makes big apple cobblers until apple season is over. If there aren't any fresh apples, she serves applesauce and apple butter for biscuits at the end of the meal. She says Benny always has to finish his meals with about three biscuits, coated with churned butter and loaded with her deep purple apple butter. When you get close to their house near mealtime, you can smell the aroma of those sweet apples cooking. Bill Sampson has to have his soup beans even when green beans are plentiful in summer. He says he can't do a day's work without a pot of beans. He covers them with onions and pepper, sops them with his cornbread and takes a little fresh ground horseradish with nearly every bite. Thelma Sampson sure knows how to cook beans with just enough salt pork simmered in. The farmers sit and eat and talk and laugh. They always get serious after a while, and then talk about crops and the weather and the cows, hogs and sheep. And they also talk about plans for the future and their dreams and how they hope for a good crop year. When dinner is over, the women are usually very pleased to see that the men have eaten so much. When you have breakfast around six in the morning after milking, and then spend six hours at hard work in all kinds of weather, it takes a big dinner to get ready for another six hours of afternoon work.

Being neighborly with Clyde hadn't been a problem as I said, but Clyde, as well as most neighbors, became upset when something was about to happen to his dog. Most will understand that if their dog has been involved in killing sheep, then the dog has to be killed. It's a touchy situation, and some don't want to believe their dog is a sheep killer.

My granddad set his gun against a fence post when he went to Clyde's. Clyde started for him, but then stopped and said, "My dog never killed any sheep and never will." My granddad then told him that if he ever saw the dog near his sheep again, he would kill it. He picked up his gun and walked over the hill toward home.

Every now and then, things do happen that upset somebody. Once in a while, a thief will come through and steal something. We had some cured hams taken out of our smokehouse a couple of years ago, but most of the time everything goes along peacefully.

During each year as the seasons change, there comes a time for everything we have to do. You hope the dog-killing times, and the disputes with neighbors don't happen often. There is plowing time, planting time, harvest time and many other times in between. There is also what you could call get-ready time, which is when work has to be done in order to get ready to plant, tend, and harvest a crop. Tobacco is the main crop for all farmers in our county. Tobacco crop money is the big payoff at the end of every year. It takes hard work to raise it, and it is a year-around job. It is planted in late spring, cultivated and tended in the summer, cut and housed in the fall, and the leaves are stripped from the stalks in early winter. The tobacco crop is finally sold at a big tobacco warehouse in December or January, and then another crop year starts all over again.

If it has been a good growing year, and the tobacco leaves cured up in a golden-brown color and silky-smooth texture, it will bring a decent price. All farmers hope that the season and the weather will allow at least some of their tobacco to be sold before Christmas. If it is, then old Santa Claus comes.

Tobacco selling day is a big day during a year. The farmers have spent nearly a year in growing it and getting it ready for this big day. If it weighs out well and sells for 40 to 45 cents a pound, then it was a good year. Farmers worry so much about droughts or wash outs and hail, which can ruin a crop, and frosts and freezes which can also ruin it. It is very important for God to send gentle rains and proper sun and dry, soft breezes for curing. Farmers will, you might say, baby each tobacco stalk and each leaf, and when everything has been done as best it can, the selling day is the reward for a year's work.

The changing seasons and the weather dictate what you do and when you do it. Work in February slows down some, but there is field work to be done during good winter days. If a farmer plans to crop on a new piece of land during the coming year, the land has to be prepared for plowing. New land is land that has not been cropped before, and has rich topsoil and grows better crops. Much of the good soil that has been cropped over and over for years is either washed away or worn out. The good days in February are a time for grubbing. Grubbing is one of the hardest kinds of work, and farmers hate to do it.

The timber has already been cut from a piece of new land, but stumps, roots, sprouts, brush, briars and rocks usually remain embedded in the earth and have to be dug out before plowing. A tool called a grub and hoe is used for this work. It is a two-bladed steel tool with a thick hoe-like blade on one side and a narrower axe-sharp blade on the other. You have to dig into the earth with the hoe blade and uncover the roots and stumps so they can be cut with the sharper blade. It is back-breaking work, but during the late February days, a worker has no problem keeping warm on a sunny hillside while grubbing, cutting, tugging and pulling all day.

The brush, roots and scraps of wood are loaded on a sled and pulled by horses to the site of a new tobacco bed and the loose rocks are thrown into a hollow or gully to prevent further washing away of the land. I like to stay home from school on tobacco bed burning day, and sometimes my granddad lets me, although not very often.

A tobacco bed is 100 feet long and 9 feet wide. After it is sown in late February or early March with tobacco seed, it is covered with a white cotton canvas to protect it from frost and severe cold. But first, the bed has to be burned in order to kill the weed seeds. The beds are usually plowed up in the fall and covered with scrub timber and tree limbs. Most of this scrap wood is drug in by a horse and a log chain when winter wood for the homes is cut in the fall. The woodpile is about five feet tall and covers the whole bed.

When the match is lit and placed into a pile of dried leaves near the center of the bed, the little spreading flames fascinate me. When I was smaller, watching the flames rise up so fast and tall would take me to another world. I'd watch it crawl under the brush and then begin to reach up through the wood with orange fingers lapping around black arms and legs and trunks, squeezing out the sap. The gray smoke would become blue, and it rose first in silence, but then you could hear it like the faint sound of a distant train coming. The colors of the flames would change fast, like many rainbows weaving and dancing together. They would go from orange to red to yellow and yellow-orange with purple strands and then to green and blue all waving to say hello, goodbye and then dying. Beneath the flaming colors, the fire talked with sizzling, snapping crackles from the wood, and snarling as a lion in wait. And the burning hickory, oak, sassafras and maple were a blend of many sweet smells, like new soap for the bath on Saturday.

I like to watch tobacco beds burn on very cold days. The colors and sounds and smells along with the heat are warming and make me feel very alive. The burning of the tobacco beds is the first thing we do to get ready for the coming growing season. The tobacco seeds are planted and covered with canvas as soon as the ground has dried out enough to work up to where it's fine and nice for the tiny seeds. The tobacco plants grow in the bed and then are set out in the fields in May and June to grow tall during the summer. Late August and September is the time to top, sucker, cut and house the tobacco. Then when the cool fall air cures the leaves, the stalks are taken down from the rails in the barn and stripped and tied in bundles. I'll explain how we do all this later. If the growing season goes well, the tobacco leaves become as valuable as a little pouch of gold.

My granddad won't let me stay home from school very often, because he feels schooling is too important. Some of the families keep their boys and some of their girls home many days a year to work, as soon as they're big enough to pitch in and help. A few of the boys from about 13 on up miss maybe a third of a school year to work.

Most of the people around here have very little schooling. They know their livelihood depends on tobacco, the sale of a few lambs or calves and the few dollars they might get from milk, cream and eggs.

When it's time to cut and house the tobacco in the fall, it's best that it be done when the tobacco has ripened to a golden yellow, and it has to be all cut and hung in the barn before the first frost. If the tobacco crop is not tended and cultivated at the right time, the only paycheck of the year could be a small one. So when the crops are ready for harvest, the kids go to the field instead of the school.

My granddad says he went to about the fourth grade. He is smart, though, and he knows so many things. He is very respected in the community and the county, and he is interested in what is happening in the world. He reads the newspaper every night from after supper around seven until he goes to bed at about nine. He can't write very well, and has a hard time putting anything down on paper. There isn't a need to do much writing anyway. He can't spell very well, and spells a word the way it sounds. He spells cattle as "kaddle." I think he knows he missed out on something very important in his life. He wants me to be in school every day, but I talk him into letting me stay home on big days when we are burning tobacco beds or on silo-filling day.

My granddad goes to a lot of meetings, and he ran for the Kentucky legislature last year and won. So he has to go to Frankfort for a few weeks at the beginning of each year to make our laws. I don't know too much about what he does there, but he seems real interested in it all. My granddad's dad was also in the Kentucky legislature way back around 1898, I think.

My great granddad came here from Hamburg, Germany when he was a small boy. He bought the farm and built the house where we now live, but he died long ago before I was born. His name was John Julius Marquardt, but his name was changed when he went into the

41

Union Army during the Civil War. He was in the infantry and was a bugler. My granddad told me that when he signed up, they wrote down Marquette instead of Marquardt, so he just kept the Marquette name from then on. I like to hear the stories about the older people.

I've also heard stories about my great grandfather on my real dad's side who fought in the Civil War for the southern side. So I had my Marquette great grandfather fighting for the north and my Cummins great grandfather fighting for the south. And they were both from the same county. I don't know, but I guess how you felt about slavery made you decide which side to fight for.

My granddad also told me that my great grandfather Marquette couldn't read until after the Civil War when he married my great grandmother Nancy Stephenson. She taught him how to read, and after he learned how to read, he wouldn't stop. My granddad said that many nights when he went to bed, my great grandfather would be reading, and that when he got up the next morning, he would still be sitting in the chair reading. He told me that when he was a boy, my great granddad would take all the boys to the hay field or tobacco or corn patch for work. My great granddad would take some books, sit under a shade tree and read all day long while the boys did the work. I always liked to hear about these stories, because it makes me think there must be something important in books.

My families sure are big ones. My granddad had 13 brothers and sisters. He married Margaret Conrad, who died before I was born, and she had 14 brothers and sisters. Her father, Frank Conrad, was born soon after his parents came here from France. I remember him, and he died about when I was six. The farms where these two families grew up were about three miles apart. The Marquette farm where I live is west of the church and store, and the Conrad place is east. And now the sons of both my great granddads own the farms and do the farming. I have so many great aunts and uncles and second cousins, that it's hard to keep up with them. That's why we keep the names, birthdays, marriages and when they die in the Bibles. One reason the families were so big was that the kids were needed for work. This doesn't seem like a good reason, but that's the way things were back then, so they tell me.

My granddad tells me some things about all the family. I'm not too interested in most of it, but some of it is interesting. He said my great granddad Conrad moved with his mother to the Short Creek area when he was a very small boy. They had nothing, but he worked hard in growing up and finally owned over a thousand acres at one time. He donated some of the land for the church when they built it a long time ago. And he said my great granddad Marquette took a wagon to Falmouth and took a big bell out of an old church there and brought it to the new church. They put it up, and I hear it ring every Sunday morning.

Many of the members of my families spread out after they grew up, but many of them live nearby and many of them farm. It can get a little lonely on a farm at times, especially during the summer when I'm not in school. But the big families stick together and keep in touch and visit each other a lot. We often have a great uncle or aunt or cousin come and spend a night or two with us. They all talk mostly about the family. When one visits us from a town or up near the big city of Cincinnati, I like to hear them talk, because they usually talk in a different kind of way and pronounce certain words differently. They usually bring a little sack of candy or something and sometimes used to bring my sister and me a balloon or a little toy. On Sundays, we often have some of our family come for dinner after church.

The main thing about big families is most of them stick together and keep up with each other. My mother gets a letter or two every week from those who live away. She has 27 uncles and aunts and 92 first cousins and she tries to keep up with all of them. I know most of them, but it's hard to keep it all straight. Sometimes though, there are disputes, and sometimes one will act in a strange way. I guess what I've learned most is that it's important to keep close. If any one of them gets real sick or needs help, there is no question that several kinfolk and neighbors will gather in to help. One time one of my great uncles, who farms down by the school, broke his back when a tree they were cutting fell down on him. The word got out that he was hurt bad, and that night there must have been 30 relatives and neighbors gathered in to see if they could help.

There is no way to explain everything about all my family, because there are so many of them, and I haven't explained anything about the Cummins side of my family, where I get my last name. This part of my family is different, because my real dad and mother divorced when I was little, and I don't see the Cummins family as much as I do some of the Marquettes and Conrads. I only get to see my real dad once in a while, which is usually in the summer. My granddad and grandmother Cummins are still living, and they live in our county seat of Falmouth. They had four boys and four girls who are my uncles and aunts. My cousin Donnie and his mother live with them, because she is divorced too. I get to go and see them every month or two, and Donnie and I have a lot of fun playing ball with some of the other town kids. We get to go to the picture show on a Saturday afternoon whenever I can get there. Donnie gets to come out and stay with me a little during the summer and we have to work, but we do get to fool around the barns and ponds and have a good time when we don't have to work. I think he gets tired of doing too much of the work, because they don't do it that much in town.

My granddad Cummins is named Juble Early, and he must have been named after Juble Early, who was a Civil War general. Some people call him Early, but most everybody calls him Judge, because he's the county judge. He was a farmer, but got tired of it and moved to town and decided to run for judge. They tell me he was the county judge back during the Depression and helped a lot of people, and people like him. He looks kind of old with all his white hair and sits in his big chair and is more easy going than my granddad I live with, who always has you doing something. So I have both grandfathers in the government now, but it doesn't mean that much to me, because I don't know too much about what they do. Neither one of them has much money, so they are not high up like a banker or rich people. It seems like we are poor in a way, because we never get to do much of anything except try to keep the farm going. We have plenty to eat, but can never buy anything at all unless we really need it.

Somebody from the Cummins family came over here from Scotland many years ago, so I must be mixed up with Scotch, French and German and maybe something else. I'm not real interested in where I came from or what mixture I am, but I keep hearing them talking about it.

It's different with both of them, but they both are high up in the county. They both seem like normal grandfathers, but I guess they have a little more spark in them than most people. They both seem interested in meetings and the government and other things. I don't think much about what they do, but sometimes think maybe I might want to get into the elections some day and be high up. I don't know, but they're always talking about what the government is doing, and I guess somebody has to do it. You can get your picture in the paper if you are in the government, but I'd rather get my picture in the paper as a great ball player. That's what I think about a lot, getting my picture in the paper. Last year, when my granddad was at Frankfort at the legislature, his picture was in the Louisville *Courier-Journal*. It was about somebody trying to buy him off, whatever that means. They said that he wasn't bought off, and everybody was talking about that you couldn't buy off Frank Marquette.

Family is important, because everything about farming is hard. It's always a struggle against nature and all that can go wrong. There is a battle to fight everyday. You have to deal with the unexpected when cows break through a fence, when the mown hay curing in the field is being threatened by dark clouds gathering in the west, when a plow point breaks, or a workhorse comes up lame. A person can't do it alone.

Things go wrong, but then it seems they start going right, if you keep working at it. Sometimes, I wish that I could do nothing, but my granddad never stops. Even when we're in the field and a big rain comes and we have to hurry to the barn, he finds something for us to do. There is always straightening up or sharpening sickle blades or fixing a wagon wheel rim. It's hard to take a resting time, because the fields and the crops aren't resting. They keep growing and changing, and if you don't stay with them, you'll lose out. When the tobacco is set out, you can't leave it alone for the summer because the weeds will take it. When the first big cutting of hay is in the barn, the stubble gains new life and the second cutting is not far behind. The farmers who fool around and don't stay with it, lose out and maybe barely make it. It's as if nature is your boss, and you have to blend in with it and work along with it as it moves, or it will pass you by. My granddad never fought against it. He knows how it all works out. And I think he knows it wouldn't work out unless he stayed right with it and kind of fit in with it to help it along. Or maybe nature helps him along, because he lets it.

The late evenings give me time to think a little by myself. I remember what I liked to do last summer during the evenings after milking and after supper. I liked to go back out to the barn and just be by myself for a while. The cows are out in the pasture behind the barn. As the sun settles toward the horizon, it gets as red as a big fire coal, but the air begins to cool everything down. As the cows slowly begin grazing and spreading out down toward the creek, their black and white colors dot the green cover of the sloping hill. After a long, hard day of pulling a plow, a disk harrow or a wagon filled with hay, the horses are eating their fill of bluegrass and clover. I like to take the harness off the horses after a day's work. They shake their bodies and are so relieved, like when I get in the tub in the smokehouse and wash off at the end of the day. The lather has built up under the harness and the collar, and when I take it off, they shake their big bodies and are so eager to get to the pond for water and then to pasture.

Being out there gives me a chance to think about everything. The barn is quiet and empty except for a few barn martins that gather in for their night's roosting. I think about the times when I was lonely and wishing that I had friends that I could see more often. It does get lonely on the farm, especially in the summertime when the crops are laid by and when my granddad has me mow briars, weeds and stubble from pasture fields all day long for many days. It gets lonely sitting on a mowing machine in the hot sun with just you and the team of horses going back and forth across a hill.

Sometimes in the summer I sit down on the big rock step in front of the corn crib and do my thinking. I think about my loneliness, but it makes me feel better to sit there in the cool for awhile, because I usually start thinking about my future and my hopes. My granddad never talks much about what I will do when I grow up. But there is a way about him that makes me believe things will be good in the future. It's hard to explain, but you felt like everything is going to be all right, because he never says or does anything to make you think your life won't be good. Each year, he just knows that his lambs will grow to be the best he ever had.

When I sit on the rock by the corn crib in the evenings, the hens that are always rambling around the barn lot work their way toward me before heading toward the hen house for their night's roost. They're fun to watch, because they strut around and cluck and look at me while waving and bobbing their heads. It's their way of asking for some kernels of corn. They disturb the quietness and my thinking, but in a way, they make me forget about loneliness or other worries. I usually take a couple of ears out of the corn crib, shell a hand-full of kernels and toss it toward the hens. After a few hand-fulls, they know it's time for the roost and work their way from the barn lot back to the hen house behind the backyard gate. When you see that you're making other things feel good, it gives you a good feeling, too.

The feeling inside sort of just happens, and you can't say this did it or that did it. It's the many little things. It doesn't seem that taking sweat-soaked harnesses off tired, hot horses would be something that would make you notice. Opening a barn door for the sheep standing out in a cold rain, or throwing a few grains of corn to the chickens are small things, but these little things begin to add up in you, and you can begin to understand that you're important. You may not be real important like people who do great things that you read about in the newspaper, but you begin to feel that you're important to all the life around you. Nobody else knows or cares too much about what you do, but if you get a good feeling inside about what you do, then it doesn't matter if nobody else knows. I do think about myself a lot when I'm alone way back on the place bringing in the cows or sitting on a mowing machine all day. But when I start thinking about how our animals and crops and fields and woods and gardens sort of all fit together, then I get that good feeling inside and don't worry much about what will happen to me. The best feeling to have is that everything is going to work out. It's about as hard to explain feelings as it is to explain how the cherry blossoms turn to sweet cherries on the tree behind the smokehouse.

In February the ground begins to thaw down into its deeper part. As the late winter sun's rays slant closer against the hills, you can see and smell the earth begin to come alive. It's like the first opening of the dairy-barn door on a cold morning. When it's opened, all is still but after the first step inside into the warmth, the barn comes alive. The animals begin stirring to greet the new day. The creaking of the door is the signal. The signals for the earth to come alive outside are small. There is no noise or sudden change, but you know it's coming. Another growing season will soon begin when the mud gets thick and the wind blows strong. It takes a warm sun and a strong wind to dry the ground. A farmer, who works the earth, must be ready and work along with nature's time. My granddad tries to be ready to plant any seed when the time is right. He never told me this, but I know, because he never waits or expects nature to change its course.

CHAPTER FOUR

THE SPRING ALARM


Grown up people don't seem to mind the weather as much as I do. Farmers are out in the weather every day, and I guess they get used to it after so many years. The bitter cold and the heat and the wet days are hard for me, especially when I have to be out during those times, but I'm getting more used to it than I used to be. Farmers have to study the weather and the way nature is, because what they do with the animals and the crops each day depends on what the weather will bring. You don't want to cut hay with rain in sight, and you don't want to miss sowing tobacco seed in the plant beds when the first warm spell arrives in the early spring. You have to know when lambs are ready to stay outside the barn at night during the late winter, and when the milk cows need to begin staying in the barn all night in the early winter. If you miss the right time, it will mess things up from then on. My granddad always says to never wait on the weather, because if you wait, you'll never get anything done. He never seems to let the weather bother him, but he knows how the weather affects every living thing. I guess you have to learn to go with it, and work with it and it somehow becomes natural so you don't need to let it bother you.

Spring can never make up its mind when to come. The other seasons seem to flow into each other, but spring is the one season that seems to hesitate and fool and tease. March is a month that is in between, and it can change fast. There are the early warm, sunny days, and you think the cold and long dreariness of winter is about over. But the cold winter winds start up again and blow dark lingering clouds over the hills. A cold, strong March wind blowing over a ridge can cut to the bone. And the March clouds can send down blowing snow, sleet or freezing rain, all mixed together at times. The weather changes quickly when the winds blow the clouds away and the sun comes out with its bright warming rays. When the ground begins to get more warming sun, and the trees begin to bud, it's the signal for a new crop year and many long, hard working days until harvest time.

I have different feelings about spring. I'm glad to see the warm days come, but also know that I won't see my friends very often when school is out in mid-May. Basketball is about over, and I will not shoot as many shots out at the rounded metal rod on the barn that one of my uncles made for me for a basket. I have a burlap sack tied with twine string for a net, and it works real well. Many cold winter days after school, or whenever I can, I shoot the basketball until the tips of my fingers chap and crack open.

Spring means baseball is coming. I see pictures in the paper of the players in spring training in Florida. I think that playing baseball there in the warm must be the grandest thing in the world. On warmer days, I get my glove and ball and go out to the barn and throw the ball way up on the barn roof and then catch it as it rolls off. I pretend that each catch is a game-saving catch at Crosley Field in Cincinnati, where the Reds play. I take my bat, which is an old broken hoe handle, and throw rocks or walnuts up in the air and hit them far down into the pasture behind the barn lot. I pretend that most of them would be home runs at Crosley Field. In the cities, they have teams for boys, and they get to play real baseball games. It must be wonderful to wear a shirt and cap of the same color for your team and play in a real game.

Last summer, on Sunday afternoons after church, Jimmy and Henry would ride their bicycles up to our place, and we'd play flies and grounders and make up other baseball games that three could play. After a couple of hours of baseball, we would ride our bicycles up to Bud Klein's store and get big cold Pepsis and candy bars. It was our treat for the week. Sunday afternoons were about the only time for much play, because the other days of spring and summer are days for work.

Although I'm glad to see the warm days begin to change the land and make it come to life, I know that spring means work. It's a crucial time for farmers, and there is much work to be done to get ready to plant the crops. February is a slack-working month, but the tobacco plant beds have been sown and covered with white canvas for protection from frost and freezes. Lettuce, radish, tomato, beet, pepper, and cabbage seeds along with onion sets are also planted at the ends of the tobacco beds. In late March, we have our first salad greens, radishes and onions. After a long winter without any fresh, garden crops, the lettuce salad mixed with chopped onions, crumpled cured bacon, and coated with hot vinegar with sugar tastes mighty good.

One of the first big jobs in early spring is hauling and spreading the manure pile that had stacked way up during the winter. The manure from 20 cows grows into a heaping pile during the winter. The cows remain in the dairy barn overnight during the winter months, and each morning the manure from the trough behind them has to be hauled out by wheelbarrow. We have a wooden ramp built up about eight feet high, and you have to push the loaded wheelbarrow up the ramp and dump it on the growing pile. It takes about five full wheelbarrow loads to clean out the barn, and it is mighty heavy when full. You have to be real careful going up the ramp, because the mushy-wet, stinking manure can splatter and get all over you. After a winter's accumulation, the manure pile is about as big as our corncrib. In mid-spring, the manure pile has to be loaded into a wagon, hauled to a field, and spread over the ground. We wear knee-high gum-rubber boots when working in the manure, but some of it still gets on you and down your boots. The manure makes very good fertilizer and is usually spread over ground that is to be planted in tobacco.

It takes many wagon loads to clean up the big pile. It is loaded into a box-bed of a wagon with a manure fork. A manure fork has five or six prongs, with the prongs set narrower together so the soft manure will not slide through. A fork full of wet, soggy manure is quite heavy, and after days of forking it, your arms ache but they become stronger for the hard summer's work ahead. A farmhand spends many days out of the year using a pitchfork with a strong hickory handle. A pitchfork for hay has three or four prongs, and tons of hay are forked to the wagons and then unloaded in haylofts or stacked in the fields during hot summer days. It takes a lot of hay to feed 20 cows, 5 horses and 120 sheep. Each farmhand has his favorite pitchfork to work with. For pitching hay, some like a three-prong pitchfork, and some liked a four-prong. I guess it's like baseball players, who have their favorite bats.

You cannot spend a day forking manure without it splattering and getting on your clothes. We get used to the smell, and actually the fresh smells of an early spring day seem to overcome the manure smell. I suppose that if a family member or someone else from town came to see us, they would get sick if they came to the manure pile while we were loading it.

When March comes and the ground is thawed out completely and dried up enough to work, it is plowing time. Breaking new ground with a hillside plow is one thing I don't have to do yet. Of course, I am in school during the day when spring plowing is done, but I also am not quite big or strong enough to follow and hold the plow as it breaks through new sod. When a plow point hits rocks, roots and stumps as it cuts through the earth, it takes a strong man to hold it and get it back into the ground. Crit and Sollie spend many a spring day breaking new ground. When I get home from school and do my chores, I like to stop by where they're plowing and watch the earth being turned. The odor of the dirt is strong, but it also has a sweet and new kind of smell, which is like a small explosion bursting open with the promise of new life and growth.

After the manure is spread, plowing ground is the next real hard work of a new crop year. It takes a while for a farm hand to get used to doing the hardest kind of work in the spring. And the horses also have to get used to it, since they aren't used to much work during the winter, especially doing long hard pulling. We have two teams of horses. Dolly and Bill have been a team for many years. Dolly is a solid gray mare, and Bill is coal black with a white face and three white feet. Jake is sorrel, and he works alongside the bay-colored Jennie. And I've told you about Lady, our saddle mare. The other horses must envy her, because she's never been harnessed. She is quite a bit smaller than the work horses and couldn't be as strong. She's never had to pull a plow, but she's covered many a mile with my granddad on her back.

Bill is my favorite workhorse. He has a beautiful color, and is slow-natured, calm and steady. Dolly can be a bit unfriendly and is contrary at times, but will always pull her share. We use Jake and Jennie whenever we need two teams. They both are younger than Bill or Dolly and are dependable, but not quite as reliable in doing tedious work like plowing through early-set tobacco or newly sprouted corn.

When you work with horses and spend time with them nearly every day, you can get close to them. I don't quite know what it is, but you gain an understanding. You get to know their nature, and they get to know yours. A horse has a nature all its own, and some are agreeable with you, and others can get cranky and balky. Bill lets me catch him out in the field when I go after all the horses in the early morning for a day's work. I carry his bridle, and walk up to him gentle like, and he usually lets me bridle him and ride him to the barn. The other horses are usually easy to drive in once they see Bill take the lead. It's easier, though, to get them to the barn if you give them a few ears of corn before harnessing. Bill is almost always gentle with me, but sometimes Dolly runs from me. She may be the smartest one after all. I guess she's probably thinking that she doesn't feel like pulling a plow all day and will just stand under a shade tree and rest.

I like the warming of spring and the changing bright colors and knowing that summer is coming when I can swim in the ponds and maybe get to go see the Cincinnati Reds play a baseball game. As I said, I have mixed feelings about the coming of spring. It's like a slow but steady alarm that goes off, calling you to the days ahead. And it's signaling that a lot of work is ahead with many long days in the hayfield or cornfield or tobacco patch.

I'm now at an age when I'm nearly big enough to do most everything on a farm. Sometimes, though, I get tired of working, especially the hardest things, or working when I'm alone. If I'm with Crit and Sollie, I know that we'll get to talk and tell stories and laugh. But I also know that I'll be alone many days mowing pastures later in the summer, and I do get lonely out on those hills all day long. I sit on that mowing machine and think about Sunday when Jimmy and Henry and I can play flies and grounders and then go get cold Pepsis at Bud's store. And I think about swimming in a real swimming pool in the city and eating ice cream cones. I think about getting to see the picture show on Saturday night if I get to go to town. My favorite cowboy is Charles Starett, who is known as the Durango Kid. I like the name Durango, because it sounds strong and brave and exciting. I also like Tex Ritter, but I don't like it when he sings too much.

Being alone also gives me time to think about myself, and I'm beginning to think about what I want to do when I grow up. It's never really worried me before, but I'm beginning to think that all the hard work and all the lonely times on the farm may not be what I want to do forever.

When I'm alone so much, I almost always begin to think about God and how much he is in charge of my life. And I wonder if he knows or really cares about what I'm doing. Whenever I'm back on our place mowing or going after the cows or chopping out tobacco, I can usually see the Short Creek Baptist Church, which is a couple of miles away as the crow flies. It sits on a high ridge, and it kind of seems as if it is watching me. Our preacher, Brother Robb, keeps telling us that God is with us and watching us all the time. But I can't figure it out. I know he is in heaven and probably watching everything I do, but heaven seems so far away, and I'm not clear about what heaven looks like with the streets paved with gold and God sitting on a throne watching and judging us. I usually try not to think about him too much, but it bothers me some, because I don't want him mad at me with the way I'm living my life.

As I said, especially whenever I'm mowing pastures and just sitting on the mowing machine all day long, I have to think about something. Dolly and Bill pretty much know how to follow along the edge of the un-mown part of the field, so there's not much to do but think until you get to the end of the field and have to turn around. You can only think so much about how you would like to be playing catch or shooting basketball or the picture show. I don't like to think too much about God, because I'm not sure how much he will rule my life or whether I will have to decide the big things on my own.

Sometimes after getting back from Bud's store on our bicycles and full of cold Pepsis and candy bars, Jimmy, Henry and I lie down under the old pear tree in the yard and talk a little about what we want to do when we grow up. Henry is two years older than me and he is a freshman in high school. He thinks about his future more than I do, and likes to talk about serious things. He's got me to thinking more about what life will be like when we leave home. I don't think too much about leaving home, because I feel like everything will work out for me.

I know that my granddad must be thinking at times about me. He has some strange ways about him, though, and never tells me anything about my life directly. And he never asks me anything about what I'm thinking. He does tell me things in a direct way, like, "I want you to mow the field behind the red barn tomorrow," or "We'll get the sheep in today." But I've heard him say many times in certain ways that he wants me to learn how to work. It seems I've always known that I must work. My granddad must strongly believe that work, "by the sweat of the brow," as the Bible says, is what a man must do. And he must feel it's his duty to teach me this important lesson. I think he knows that if a boy, early on, is taught to work, then he has something that can take him on to many other things later. He's never told me this, but he has shown me.

Another thing about my granddad is that after a day's work and supper, when he picks up the paper or something else to read he acts like there is nobody around him. You can see the serious look on his face. It's not a worried look, but almost like a peaceful look. I could always tell how he respected anyone who had learned so much from books and school.

The books are over for me in mid-May when school is out, and it is a big change. I am beginning to read a few books and more of the paper in the summer time. The change comes when, rather than sitting at a desk with papers and books, I'm out in a field with a hoe, a pitchfork or a pair of check lines in my hands to drive the horses. We boys kind of get tired of school when the days get longer and the sun shines brighter, but it takes some time to get used to working every day.

One of the first big jobs around mid-May and usually after school is out is sheep shearing. Of course, the sheep need their thick heavy coat for the winter, but they need it sheared off for the coming hot days of summer. It's a job I don't like, because I have to hand-turn the crank of the shearing machine. It's like turning the crank of an ice cream freezer, except ice cream freezes in about 15 minutes, but shearing takes three or four days. Standing there and turning that crank all day long is sure a lot different than learning my spelling words at school.

Not many farmers, tenants or hired hands can shear sheep very well, so we hire Big Jess Jacobs to shear ours. He can shear three or four while Crit or Sollie are shearing one. The wool is sold, and it brings in a little money that helps out during the spring of the year. I do like to take the tied bundles of wool from each sheep and pitch them up into a big burlap sack tied to a tobacco rail up in the barn. The sacks are about 12 feet long, and I pitch the big wool balls into the sacks and then climb up and get into the sack and trample and pack the wool tightly down into the sack.

The sheep look funny after being sheared as they run from the barn out into the crisp spring air. Their woolly coat would be up to about four inches thick, and when it is sheared down next to their skin, the sun shines against the white fuzzy layer and makes it appear as if they have on a cape of gold.

Big Jess is a rough man. He shears sheep for many farmers in the spring, but doesn't do much else during a year. He wears bib overalls and rolls around on the dirt barn floor with the sheep as he shears them. The oil from the wool makes the front of his blue overalls black and slick, and the urine and manure stains other parts of his clothes. My mother doesn't like having Big Jess eat dinner with us, but all hired hands eat dinner with the boss man on a farm. Big Jess doesn't have many table manners. He slurps and belches and picks at his teeth with a fork. Gravy drops from his bread and slides down the slick, black oily layer on his overalls. He doesn't change clothes until after sheep shearing time is over. If he has a big, fresh chew of tobacco in his mouth at dinnertime, he takes it from his mouth and puts it in his shirt pocket. The brown juice seeps through and his shirt gets stained a dirty brown in front, but remains a salty blue-white everywhere else. After we finish eating and sit at the table and rest for a few minutes, Big Jess takes the chew from his pocket and plops it in his mouth. When it is about time for him to spit, my granddad says that it's time to head back to the barn. My mother probably dislikes sheep shearing time as much as I dislike turning the hand crank that makes the clippers slide through the wool.

A field of newly sheared sheep with their new white coats glistening in the sun is a sign that summer is near. The hills have also discarded one coat for another. The brown stubble cover on the ground has turned to a light yellow-green. The sheep move slowly down over the hill and nibble at the fresh new sprigs. My granddad often leans against the gate and watches the white dots disappear into the late evening, knowing that he too has to put away his old warm coat as summer is coming.

There is something about spring I don't like. It's cold rains and blustery, windy days. The warm, sunny spells can suddenly turn into cold and wintry ones. A light snow or sleet in April is not a welcome sight, and it always makes me want to skip those uncertain days. It's often too warm to have a fire in the house, but too cool to not have one. You can get too warm working with a jacket on, but too cool without one. There is just something about spring that gives me an uneasy feeling.

Maybe my feeling about it has something to do with Easter. The lessons I learn at Short Creek Baptist Church are all good ones and most are happy, except I still don't know if God is mad at me. Our preacher, Brother Robb, sometimes gets all worked up about sin and says that it is harder to get into heaven than it is for a camel to go through the eye of a needle. I don't want a hard life, but it sure seems like everything is a struggle sometimes. I just don't have a good feeling about Easter when Jesus was crucified. They say he did it for our sins, but I don't understand why God put him through all that. We used to get cards every Sunday with pretty Bible pictures on the cover and a lesson inside. I never liked the one at Easter showing Jesus suffering on the cross, with that awful expression on his face. The crown of thorns and the blood and his pierced side just leaves me with a bad feeling. I want everything to be good and warm and happy. I don't like for people to be mad at each other. I don't even like to see my granddad or Crit get mad at Bill when he steps on a plant of tobacco when we're plowing. They don't get mad very often, but sometimes when a workhorse or a milk cow gets flighty and acts a little crazy they get disgusted. It seems like sometimes people get flighty too, and act bad.

It must be the picture of Jesus on the cross that causes me to not like Easter like the other holidays. The nails that were driven through his hands are the worst part of it all. When Easter Sunday is blustery and rainy, that makes it seem like Jesus suffered even more if he died on a dreary, cold day.

Some Easters are warm and sunny, and that makes it better and brighter. Like other holidays, we usually have some relatives come stay with us overnight, and they usually bring my sister and me a bag or basket of candy. And there are always the Easter egg hunts, which were very exciting when I was younger.

At school on the Friday afternoon before Easter, the teachers would let us go out in the big school yard that ran back a ridge surrounded by Calvin Jackson's bushy farm and have an Easter egg hunt. Everyone always had plenty of hard-boiled eggs, colored up real pretty, and they would be scattered and hidden all around the grounds.

The boys would sometimes have contests to see who could eat the most boiled egg yolks. We'd also usually get some chocolate eggs, and all the yellow-green egg yolks mixed with the chocolate never settled well with me.

My mother fixes a special meal for our family visitors on Easter morning. The Easter breakfast is special, because it is the first one of the year when we cut a new cured country ham. My granddad takes one down from the curing rafter in the smokehouse and it looks moldy when you take it from the cloth sack, but he trims off the moldy part and slices it into big thick slabs. The dark red meat of a new country ham tastes so good, and of all the smells in our kitchen, frying cured ham is the best. It's not like any other smell. It is strong, but yet sweet. You can smell the curing blend of salt, pepper, and brown sugar all together, as it cuts right through the air with the coffee boiling and the sweet biscuits baking, each giving off their own strong and sweet smell. But the ham has its own stout way and makes every other cooking smell seem weak. It makes you hungry, and when you're coming in from milking at the barn and sitting by the fire with a big plate of ham, eggs and biscuits, you'd be ready for a long day in the field. For Easter breakfast, my mother fries up a big platter of the thick red ham slices and fries up a dozen or more eggs in the reddish-brown ham grease. White biscuits, ham gravy, churned butter, blackberry preserves and sorghum molasses top off our Easter breakfast along with plenty of sweet milk and hot black coffee. I usually get kind of a sick feeling at breakfast, though, because of too much Easter candy, which I am not used to eating.

Maybe it's the sick feeling that causes me to have some unhappy thoughts of Easter. But I really think it's the suffering on the cross, and the sadness it leaves me. My granddad never talks about suffering. If he ever suffered, he'd never let on. He never talks about God, but every Sunday morning after milking, he comes in, gets cleaned up and sits down for a while and reads his Sunday School lesson and a little bit of the Bible. You can tell he's thinking about what he's reading, but he never says anything about it. He always has a serious look on his face when he's reading his lesson, just as he always has a serious look on his face when he's with his sheep. But he seems more at ease with his sheep than he does at church. He understands everything about his sheep. But maybe he is like me and hasn't figured out how God and Jesus have plans for us. It would be better if we could feel good and easy in church. I don't think he feels good until he gets home, puts on his work clothes, walks out to the barn and looks down over the fields at his cattle and his sheep.

When the days gradually become warmer and longer and the sun becomes brighter, the earth seems like it's going through a slow, silent explosion. The grass and all plants begin to come to life. Under the white canvas of the tobacco beds, the ground is warmer which helps to sprout the tobacco plants quicker. One plant bed provides enough plants to set about an acre and a half of tobacco. I explained to you earlier about how we burn a bed in order to kill the weed seeds. But the burning does not kill all the weed seeds, and many of them sprout along with the tobacco seeds. If the weeds are left to grow in the beds, they will overtake the tiny tobacco plants and choke them out.

We have to weed the beds at the right time. It is a tedious job, and I don't like to do it, and don't have to help except on a Saturday or sometimes after school. It is the only job I know of that we have to lie down to do. We fill a big burlap sack with straw, put it out on the bed, lie down on the sack, and with our fingers, pick each little weed out from around the tobacco plants. New little tobacco plants are very delicate and smaller than a dime when we go in and weed around them. It's important that you not step on the bed or pull or damage a newly sprouted tobacco plant. Each tobacco plant is precious, and it is nourished and cared for from the time the seed is sown in early spring until the time the stalk is stripped of its leaves in the winter and taken to market. Any plant and any animal that is sold is handled in a special way, because it means the money will be a little more at the end.

Many farmers learned how to farm from their fathers. And the way they did things was not always the best way. My granddad tries to keep up with doing things the best way. He was always interested in the news back during the war, and he studied what our president and other politicians were saying. He tries to keep up with better ways of raising crops, fattening lambs and getting the cows to give more milk. Tobacco, lambs, wool, and milk are sold by the pound, and the more pounds there are, the more money comes in. He talks with the county agriculture agent a lot, and the county agent sends him papers from the government or the University of Kentucky agriculture experiment station, which explains many ways of improving the way things grow. Many of the neighbor farmers don't understand that the county agent can help them. Most of them don't read much of anything or just don't trust new ways. Their daddies taught them, and that is good enough,

My granddad takes pride in a stall full of fat lambs or a barn full of golden-brown tobacco. He doesn't brag like some of the farmers do when they talk a little outside after church on Sunday morning. After the preacher shakes your hand at the door, the men gather over at the side of the churchyard under a walnut tree. Most of them roll and light a cigarette or put in a chew, and talk for a few minutes before going home to Sunday dinner. It is the one time of the week when the farmers can find out how far along each of them are with their crops. Of course, we always know who the braggers are. Farmers like Louis Wiggins will say things like, "How big are your plants, Frank?" And he'll say about the size of a dime. And Louis will take a big puff and say something like, "Oh, I've got em bigger than a quarter," but we know it probably isn't true.

It seems to give my granddad satisfaction to see things doing well. I don't think it's always the money. He just seems to be pleased in a quiet sort of way to see everything healthy and growing in a natural way as it ought to be. He spends a lot of time planning ahead. The work comes about as the seasons and the weather changes. You have to be ready to break ground at the right time, and to plant garden at the right time, and to cut tobacco at the right time. Most of the planning is already in place, and that is the way most farmers work, and just do it when it's time. It doesn't take a lot of thinking to do it this way. My granddad likes to be a step ahead.

He's always one of the first in the county to try a new idea sent down by the university experiment station. Doing those things takes more time at first, but he can see the benefit in the long run. We were one of the first around to dope our sheep and to castrate our buck lambs a new way. At the end, the paychecks are important, but my granddad takes pride everyday in trying to do it all the right way.

It's not always an easier way, because we are always doing extra stuff, it seems to me. I get tired of fooling with the sheep so much. When I was younger, I had more time to play, and my granddad wouldn't make me be with them all the time. But whenever there was something I could help with, I had to be with them, and now I have to be with them most all the time. A lot of days I'm beginning to kind of wish I had more time to do what I want to do. But it's fun to be with Crit and Sollie and the other farm hands we have from time to time. It's more fun to be doing something where we can laugh and talk, but my granddad has always said that you "can't talk and work at the same time." He's never real hard on me, but I've always tried to do what he tells me. I was brought up to just go ahead and do it. I usually get a little time at the end of a day to shoot my basketball at the hoop on the barn. Then I can believe I'm in a game at Morgan High School and wearing one of their beautiful gold uniforms. That satin gold shirt must feel mighty good on your skin, and they're so pretty with the blue numbers. I wonder what number I'll get when I'm on the team in a couple of years? I think I would like wearing either 3 or 8. People will be watching then, and now every time I hit a long shot at the barn, I can hear them cheer for me. Whenever I get tired of doing the work, I start thinking about hearing people cheer for me, and it makes me feel good to know that someday it will happen.

After the sheep have been out in the pasture for a month or so, we round them all up, bring them to the barn and dope every ewe and ram. The county agent told us about a new chemical that rids the sheep of stomach worms and other parasites. It's called phenothiazine. My granddad could never read or say big words very well, and he calls it something like feenix-izeen. It's a chalky, dark-green mixture and must taste very bad to the sheep. We take a big metal syringe with about a cup of the liquid mixture in it, catch and straddle a ewe, force the six-inch part into the sheep's mouth and down its throat, and squirt the stuff into its stomach. It's a rough job, and after wrestling around with more than a hundred sheep, we are always glad when that job is over.

There are many things a boy can't do, but there comes a time when I have to try everything the first time. It takes a man to catch and straddle a strong, scared ewe and squirt the dope into its stomach. Last year when we were doping the sheep, my granddad handed me a loaded syringe, and told me to do one. Crit and Sollie sort of stood back and grinned. I was a little scared, but grabbed a scampering ewe around the neck, slung my leg over its back and tried clamping its mouth with my free hand while raising its head up to force in the syringe. The ewe lunged and bucked and off I went right down into the soggy manure on the stall floor. The other ewes spooked and several ran over top of me. Crit, Sollie and my granddad laughed and laughed. It hurt my feelings a little, because I couldn't hold her, but my granddad said, "You'll be able do it next time." I don't think he was trying to embarrass me, he was only trying to push me a little toward being a man.

When we finish doping the bucks and ewes, we also have to castrate the buck lambs and cut the tails off all the lambs. I know it is best for the lambs in their growth, but it hurts me some to do it. We used to have to catch a lamb and hold it up so that one of the men could cut its tail off, and then if it was a little buck, cut its bag off at the end and squeeze its two nuts out and throw them away.

When it's time to castrate, the lambs are about two to three months old, and they are very cute and frisky and playful at that age. Now that I'm telling about it, it seems like cutting their nuts out is cruel and bad. You have to get used to blood, dirt, mud and manure and never worry about getting any of that kind of stuff on you. I never liked piss and manure on my clothes, but blood is the worst to me. My granddad goes on like it's nothing. The worst part of it all is hearing the little lambs cry.

We used a very sharp pocketknife to do the cutting the old way. Every farmer keeps his pocketknife razor sharp for many things. When the cut was made, the blood squirted everywhere, and sometimes up on your face if you weren't careful in how you held the lamb. After the cut, we'd take a rag and dab a mixture of turpentine, coal oil and pine tar on the cut to help stop the bleeding and also help heal it. When I'd let a little lamb down, it would act kind of pitiful and stagger and fall and cry. I'd want to go to it and try to help it, but would have to hurry and catch another lamb, because the sooner this whole thing was over with, the better.

The cutting sometimes caused too much loss of blood, and sometimes flies would get into the cut and cause it to fester. We then started burning the tails and bags off, because the wound didn't bleed near as much and it healed faster. We would build a hot bonfire outside the barn and heat up the metal part of a tool that looked something like a long, wide chisel. When it was red hot, I'd catch a lamb, set it down on a block of wood, and one of the farm hands would push the hot metal to the tail or bag and burn it off. The smell always made me a little sick. The singed, burnt wool and flesh gave off an awful smell, but after awhile you'd get used to it. I don't know if it hurt the lambs as much as cutting, but it was better for them in the long run.

After the war, more and better tools came along, and my granddad was always looking for something better. We started using a new tool called an elastrator to castrate and cut the tails off the lambs. It's something like a pair of pliers, and it has four prongs at the end. You put a very strong rubber band about the size of a coat button over the prongs and squeeze the handles. The rubber band opens up enough to slip over the bag or tail. When it's put over the bag, you have to be sure that both nuts are below the rubber band. Then you release and slip the tool away from the lamb. The strong rubber band squeezes very tight as the lamb is let go. The little lambs jump and cry and shake as if trying to shake the rubber band off. In a little bit, they just lie down and act real sick.

After their mothers are turned back with them, they get up slowly and nurse a little, and then move off down over the hill in the pasture field. In a couple of weeks, the tails and bags drop off and there is no blood or swelling or infection. The sheep are ready for the summer. There is no need to bring them into the barn again until weaning time.

My granddad rides Lady out nearly every day to look at them. He often wants me to go with him in case we need to change pastures or if I need to go into the bushes to look for a stray, a lost lamb or one that's in trouble. He often sets up on top of a ridge and calls for them in a sing-song way to come out of the shade just so he can look at them and check on them. "Sheepy, sheepy, oh, sheepy, sheepy, now sheep, ooo, sheeeeeep!" In a way, it's funny to hear him use this high-pitched voice. It sounds like Daisy Northcutt singing a hymn at church. But the sheep know his voice, and they begin baaing and baaing and coming to him. He takes along a sack of crushed corn or a little salt and spreads it on the ground for them. He knows that if they get a treat, they'll learn to come at his call. If everything is all right, he doesn't say anything, but I know he feels good about it all.

# CHAPTER FIVE

## THE GROUND IS READY

When I was in the third grade, I remember waking up the morning after school was out in mid-May, and I had a terrible feeling. As soon as I woke up, I felt so lonesome and I wanted to see Miss Thompson, my teacher. She was really pretty and much younger than the other three teachers at Goforth School. She had on perfume each day and smelled so good. And she had on lipstick and rouge and wore pretty flowered dresses. I liked her very much and always tried to do my lessons as best I could, so that she would say how good I was. She was hard with her lessons, but she had a way about her that made me want to be real close to her and to touch her. She was something like a frisky colt in the way she would just make everything seem so happy, even the lessons. It's hard to explain now that I look back on it, because I don't really know why I was so sad that morning, but it made me want to cry. I wanted to be back with her that much.

Now that I'll soon be 13, and can do about as much work as a man, I still get those lonely feelings when school is out, but when the ground is about ready for planting, you don't have much time to think about loneliness or sadness or anything else.

One of our neighbors, Bunk Wadsworth, always says, "What you do in June is what counts," and he's right. June is one of the busiest months. Although the late spring air is still fresh and clean, the days heat up fast. June mornings are usually cool, but by dinnertime the sun is bearing down, and the heat takes some getting used to. And as the days get longer, the workday gets longer. We milked our cows at around 5:00 or 5:30 in the afternoons during winter when it started getting dark. But as the summer comes around, we're still in the field at that time, because we have to take advantage of the daylight. It's usually 7:00 or later before we're through at the barn in the summer.

The ground has to be worked real good just before planting time. With the plowing done in March or April, the new-turned earth has had a month or so to kind of smooth out under heavy spring rains and frosts and some freezes. The first disking of the plowed ground in late May or early June is rough to do. It shakes your innards loose. The disk harrow has about 12 sharp rounded discs or wheels that are curved and slanted to cut up the ground as the horses pull the harrow over the rough ground. The first disking cuts through the sod and the high lumpy earth and smoothes it out a little. Whenever the discs hit a root or a rock or a deep gully, it can throw you off the harrow seat. It's so rough that we always tie a cured sheepskin to the seat to make it softer on your rear-end. Sometimes if the ground is too rough and bumpy, we pull the harrow with three horses instead of two, because it is so hard on them.

After the first disking, the ground is still rough and lumpy, but has smoothed out some. We then have to drag or rub the ground. You might not understand what I'm trying to describe, and I know city folks don't know much about farm work and the tools we use, so I'll try to explain it as best I can. A drag is about eight feet wide and is made of four or five logs tied and nailed together. The horses pull it across the ground to smooth it out more and to crumble the clods. You can either ride the drag standing up or walk behind it. If you ride it, sometimes it will throw you off when it hits a big rock, root or stump. We throw the rocks on the drag and then throw them off at the end of the field, usually in a hollow or gully.

After the ground has been rubbed or dragged after the first disking, it then has to be disked again. Sometimes it has to be disked three or four times before it's ready for planting. Corn ground doesn't have to be as smooth and fine as tobacco ground. But you want your tobacco ground as smooth as you can get it, because the tobacco crop is the most important thing you have. If it turns out to be a bad crop year, then it may mean trouble to make all the payments at the end of the year.

Whenever we go to church or town, my granddad is always looking to see what the neighbors are doing and how well they are getting along. Driving down the road, he might say, "Tom needs to disk that ground one more time," or "Louis never did have his ground ready on time." He is always kind of studying the situation, thinking about what needs to be done, and when it's best to do it when the time comes.

I'm not really interested in what he's interested in. As I grow older, I think more about playing ball with Jimmy and Henry on Sunday afternoons and going to high school and playing for the Morgan Raiders. But I can see how he gets me to learn about what we have to do. When he says, "Tom needs to disk that ground one more time," I know that our ground will be as fine as powder before planting time. Everything he says seems to be important, and he doesn't keep carrying on about it.

I know I've talked about the weather a lot, but in late spring and before planting time, you have to work with the weather. Of course you can't work ground until it's dry enough and just right. And when it is, you have to stay with it. Showers and rain come often in the spring. If it looks like rain is coming, it might mean disking till dark. When spring comes, the teachers don't assign as many spelling words or arithmetic problems at night. They know the kids all have more work to do after school to get ready for planting time. And if it's been a rainy time and work is backed up, some of the boys have to stay home from school to help get caught up with work.

As this important time of the year comes closer, after the preaching service at church, the men talk about their tobacco plants and how they're getting along. You'll hear things like, "My plants are pushing the canvas," or "We'll be settin' in a week." It seems like you can see the tobacco plants grow in the warm moist earth under the white canvas. As the plants near five or six inches in height, it means that you better have your ground ready.

If a neighbor's plants aren't ready yet and ours are, we sometimes trade work at setting time. A neighbor and maybe his kids will come and help us, and then we'd go and help him when his plants are ready. It's more fun this way, because I get to be with other people and hear different stories. And if the kids come, there might be a little time to play at dinner time or when the men take a little break at the end of a row to take a smoke.

It seems like everything comes at once during certain times of the year. Not only is setting out tobacco plants and planting corn seed one of the most important times of the year, but it is also the time for putting up the first cutting of hay. Making garden comes at the same time. I guess you can see why Bunk says that what you do in June is what counts. When the nights begin to warm up, the hills come alive. Everything grows so fast, you have a hard time keeping up with it. The hay needs to be cut at the right time, because if you wait too long, it might not have time to grow enough to get a second cutting. And you never know how bad the winter is going to be, so you want to get plenty of hay stored away for the worst kind of winter.

Since tobacco brings in the biggest paycheck at the end of the year, we have to give it the most attention. As I said, when the plants grow to about six inches, they are ready to set in the field. Of course, the ground has to be ready and smooth and fine, but the real important thing is the season. What we call the season means that it has rained enough to soak the ground so the plants live when they are set out. You can't set the plants in dry dirt, because they won't live. So you wait until the rains come. I've been dropping tobacco plants since I was six years old. All the tenant farmer's kids drop plants. I don't think any kid likes to do it, but it has to be done.

When everything is just right, we go to the tobacco beds, pull the plants, load them into a wagon and head for the tobacco patch. The kids take a big bundle and drop a plant about every three feet apart on the rows that have been laid off through each patch. The men then set the plant into the rain-soaked ground. It is very hard work, because they have to stay bent over all the time. They take two fingers, poke them into the ground, place a plant in the hole and then pack the earth around the plant. You have to keep moving, because if you don't, it will take forever. The plants have to be set just right with the moist dirt packed firmly around the roots or they won't live. My granddad is real particular about setting tobacco the right way.

We kids get muddy and wet from carrying the plants, but after awhile, you get used to it. The men are almost too tired to go milk after bending over all day in the hot sun. And their fingers are cut and scratched and split open. When you stick your fingers in the ground thousands of times, sharp rocks are going to cause some damage. A few of the older men use a wooden peg to stick in the ground, but that way is too slow, and most men think it's too sissy to use a wooden peg. A farmer's hands stay pretty tough. My granddad's hands are as tough and hard as a dried piece of leather. Nothing seems to bother him when he has to take hold of anything. In another year, I'll be ready to set tobacco, and I know it's going to be hard, because my hands aren't very tough yet.

Some of the farmers are beginning to use a jobber to set tobacco. Since the war, they've come out with better and easier ways to do many things. The jobber can be used while standing up. It's made out of light metal and has two sections to it and two handles. One side of the jobber holds about three gallons of water, and the other side has a chute where you drop the plant. As the setter and the dropper walk down a row, the dropper drops a plant in the chute while the setter pushes the jobber in the ground. He then presses a spring-loaded button to let some water drop down onto the roots of the plant that is down in the ground. When he lifts the jobber out of the ground, the dirt closes in around the plant, and it usually lives pretty well. We'll probably start setting our tobacco this way, because you don't have to wait on a good rain before setting it out.

At the end of a hard, hot day of tobacco setting, the plants are wilted and all drooped over. They look like they could never live. But the next morning, they'll be sticking up all fresh like, and when my granddad rides Lady out to take a look he'll be satisfied.

As I've said before, tobacco is very important, because it brings in most all of our money for the year. Corn is also very important, because it keeps all our animals alive and healthy during the winter. We grow three kinds of corn. One is field corn and one is what we eat and the other is silage corn. We use the ears of field corn for all the animals. We use it to fatten our meat hogs, and shell a few ears each day for the chickens. The chickens follow you around the barnyard clucking away and hoping for some kernels. I like to stop by the corncrib, take a couple of ears, shell it by hand and throw it out to them. You can almost feel their appreciation. At dinnertime, we always water and feed our workhorses first before going to the house. After a hard morning in the field, throwing five or six ears in their feed box makes them mighty happy. And in the winter, when you give the milk cows a big scoop shovel heaping with sweet-smelling silage topped with a can of crushed corn, you know their bags will be bursting with milk the next morning.

Corn ground doesn't have to be worked as fine as tobacco ground and disking it a couple of times is usually enough. We plant about two acres of field corn so the sheep, cows, horses and chickens have ears and kernels to eat, but it takes about ten acres of silage corn to fill our big silo. We use a hand corn planter to plant the seeds, and it doesn't take the time or pains that it takes to get the tobacco set out.

A few of the neighbors still take shelled corn to the mill to grind their own meal for cornbread, but we now just buy a sack of meal every now and then. Our tenant farmers use a lot of corn meal. It's cheaper than flour, and they eat a lot of cornbread with milk gravy or soak it in buttermilk and fill up that way. We also used to grow a little wheat to take to the mill for flour, but now we buy a 25-pound sack of flour at a time, because it's so much easier. Some of the farm women bake up enough biscuits to last for breakfast, dinner and supper. My mother usually bakes enough for one meal at a time. I suppose that's the way she wants to do it. A hot biscuit is much better than one that has been left on the table and covered with a cloth for the next meal. She bakes yeast rolls on Sundays or when people come visit for a meal. Whenever we have the preacher, he always brags about her rolls, and sometimes he eats so many I don't see how he can preach the evening sermon.

We spend a lot of time working in the cornfields, hayfields and the garden, and my mother and sister are always working with food in the kitchen. About all we do everyday is work to feed ourselves and take care and feed all the animals. With all the animals we keep, it takes a lot of corn and hay to feed them. We work all summer to put up the hay and get the corn in the crib and fill the silo. You feed the horses so they can do the work, which is plowing, disking, mowing, raking and pulling the wagons and sleds. It takes a lot of the hay and silage to feed the cows and sheep all through a winter. And all this work brings in a little check each month for the milk and a check from the sale of the lambs in the summer. We slop the hogs, feed the chickens, make the garden, can the beans and berries and sausage just so everything has enough food to eat. It all seems kind of natural, and nobody ever stops and asks why it must be done. It's like an old dog out hunting all day for a rabbit to eat. He doesn't think about it, but just hunts when he's hungry, which is nearly every day.

The hay fields have grown high and thick by tobacco-setting time, so it's important to get the first cutting in the barn when it's ready. I've been mowing since last year, and it's a job that let's me think about things. I just sit there and go across the field and let the sickle cut through the hay. That's about it, because the horses know to stay close to the hay that is standing. When they get to the end of the field, they know to stop and wait for me to make the turn. But I have to pay some attention, because the horses can get contrary at times and stray off.

I never wear a shirt in the summer. It's cooler to me without one, and my back gets as brown as an acorn. When mowing and riding back and forth across a hill all day in the hot sun, I get drowsy and dreamy, but I have to keep going and pay some attention. I know when I finish a field and have done it faster than my granddad thought I could, he will be pleased. He's never too pleased, though, because I guess he wants to get everything done on time and doesn't want to be too far behind the way some of the neighbors are. He acts like sometimes he wants me to do more than I can. I've heard him say many times that a boy has to be taught to work. And as I told you before, I've heard him say many times that you can't talk and work. He wants you to keep your mind on what you're doing. His tenant and hired hands know this from the start, and they don't move to our farm if they're afraid of work. I've heard talk many times about somebody being afraid of work. I think this means that you're not actually afraid, but that there is only one way to work, and that is to go at it all the time.

Whenever I get too dreamy out mowing, something usually happens that wakes me up. Sometimes I'll be mowing along and a big old blue racer snake will come streaking out of the grass. And sometimes I'll cut into a rabbit nest with little ones. It makes me sad to cut the leg off a rabbit, especially a baby one. About all you can do is stop the mowing machine, get off and hit the mangled rabbit in the head with a rock to put it out of its misery. Sometimes I'll be mowing along and one of the horses will start jumping and squirming. It's usually a horsefly up on the rump biting and drawing blood. You can take the check line and try to knock the horsefly off without stopping the mowing machine. When horseflies get real bad, you have to stop, go up to the rear of the horse and kill the fly with your hand.

There is no question that if you get too dreamy out mowing a field, a nest of yellow jackets will wake you up. You can be mowing along without much happening and then maybe the horses start jumping and even running. When this happens, you know the sickle has run into a yellow-jacket nest. The only thing you can do is jump off the mowing machine and start running, because the yellow jackets have first attacked the horses and you will be next. Their sting is mighty painful. You get used to sweat bees, and their sting hurts a little, but not for long, but yellow jackets can knock you off the

70

mowing-machine seat. They're like the Jap suicide pilots in the war, the way they dive down after you.

I never wear a shirt in the summertime as I said, so my back is a good target. And you never see yellow jackets coming. Bill, Dolly and I were mowing along one hot day when we must have hit a real big nest. They went after me first, because the horses hadn't jerked or spooked. I don't know how many hit me, but it must have been a dozen all at the same time. I threw the check lines down and ran away as fast as I could, but they still came after me. It almost made me sick. I had many welts on my back, and after things settled down and they finally flew away, I went back to mowing, although I didn't feel very good from all the poison under my skin. My granddad never let anything stop him from work, and I think it probably rubbed off on me.

We do get a day or part of a day off now and then. Of course, we never work on Christmas Day except for the milking and feeding morning and night. On Thanksgiving Day, we usually strip tobacco during the morning, but stop for the big turkey dinner at noon and then hunt during the afternoon. The Fourth of July is another day we don't have to work, and I'll tell you about this day later. We also usually take part of the day off on Decoration Day. Many of my great uncles and aunts and second cousins and others come back to the home place on this day.

The home place is where we live and where my whole family on my mother's side started. My granddad bought the farm around the time of World War I. His dad bought it after the Civil War, and built the house we live in, and raised all of his 14 kids here. I often wish I had some brothers, so I would not get so lonely at times, but not 14. Most all of my granddad's 13 brothers and sisters moved away from the farm when they grew up, and many of them live in town or in or near Cincinnati. Many of them always come back on Decoration Day in very nice clothes and sometimes bring a little candy or gifts for us when they came. I like to have them visit, because they tell us about how they live. They get to go to a picture show almost whenever they want to and get ice cream and soft drinks whenever they want, and they have bathrooms and refrigerators for ice.

When they come, my mother has a big dinner and then they usually go out in the yard and pick flowers. My mother has a lot of different kinds of flowers in the yard. We then take the flowers to the Short Creek Cemetery. They get out of the car and go to the tombstones of our buried relatives and put the flowers on the mound of dirt and just stay quiet and stand there for a while. I don't like this part of the day, because I don't want to think about dead people. I try not to think about when you die. I've seen a few dead people lying in a casket, an old great aunt, a neighbor girl who died young and a few others. It makes me feel real sick-like when they just lie there and don't move. My mother talks to me about dying sometimes, but it's because she's afraid I'll get hurt out climbing way up in the rafters of the tobacco barn or way up in the silo. I heard her tell my granddad many times when I was younger to not let me hitch up the horses, because we've had neighbors kicked in the head by a horse or gored by a bull. And she always worries about catching flu in the wintertime. A few years ago, one of our tenant's little girls died from the flu. It was so sad. A big drifting snow was on and they had to bring her little body out to the road with a horse and sled. Dying does scare me, so I try not to ever think about it.

Nearly every day I see my granddad wring the head off a frying chicken, and I've seen many dead dogs and varmints lying out in a field. And at hog-killing time, when Crit takes a 22 and hits a fat hog between the eyes, it makes me a little weak, but you get used to seeing dead animals all the time. After the hog hits the ground, my granddad jumps in and sticks his sharp butcher knife right in the hog's throat, and the blood sometimes squirts three or four feet high. If blood squirts on him, he doesn't seem to mind. Well, it does cause me to still act a little shy about it all, and I don't know if I'll ever really like it.

At the cemetery, when all the flowers have been placed on the graves and there's been a little quiet talking, we get back in the cars and begin talking about good things again and laughing. When we get back home, the men sit out in the yard under the old pear tree, and the women sit inside or on the front porch and talk. The kids then get to run and play a little, and it's fun again when we don't have to think about graves and dying for awhile.

The kinfolks usually get ready to go back home about the time we have to go milk. Sometimes they stay a little while longer and go to the barn to watch us. Sometimes the city kids go with me to bring in the cows from the pasture. It's funny how they are. They don't know the first thing about driving in a herd of cows. They usually have on their good shoes and will step right in a big cow pile if they're not watching, and that is really funny. One time, one of the city women came out to the barn when I brought the cows in. In the summertime, the cows always go to the pond to drink before going in the barn, and some of them will wade way out in the pond before drinking. When she saw them out in the water, she said, "Is that where the cows take their baths?" My granddad thought that was one of the funniest things he ever heard, and he told that story many times later.

When my kinfolk from the towns and cities visit, it shows that they don't know much about the farm or nature. When they leave, we go back to the way we always live. I can be with them one day laughing and talking, and then the next day, I'm back with the horses or out in a field thinking about many things about my life. It can be a lonesome time, and my mind sort of scatters around thinking about the fun you can have with people. When people are not around, though, you have to try to keep a good feeling.

Many times when I'm wondering about everything, I go back to how God fits in. The preachers are always talking about how if you let Jesus in your heart, he'll always be with you and protect you and you'll never be lonely again. When I get to thinking about all this, it's hard to think he's sitting on the mowing machine with me out in a hay field. I then wonder if he gets up and goes someplace else when the yellow jackets fly in, and if it's punishment for my sins. The best way to keep from trying to figure it out is get your mind back on a tobacco patch and a hay field.

When it's planting time, tobacco comes first. Corn planting is worked in between tobacco setting and haying. By the time the tobacco is out and started, the clover fields have grown thick and high and are falling over. And getting the first cutting of hay in the barn takes many a day's work. After a couple of days of drying and curing in the sun, it's ready to be raked, loaded on a wagon, and hauled to the barn. My granddad does the raking. He usually does more of the sitting-down jobs now that he is getting older and his lumbago bothers him more all the time.

The sweet-smelling cured hay is raked by a team pulling a big-wheeled rake, which has about 20 curved teeth attached to a ten-foot wide frame. New mown hay has a clean, fresh smell, and cured hay in the field has a tender, sweet smell. It's not like flowers or the strong-sweet smell of moist corn silage. It smells better than the perfume you smell when you get close to the ladies' Sunday school class at church. It smells clean out in the sun and fresh when the dew has covered it in the early mornings. No wonder the cows chomp down on it on a cold winter's day. We rake it into what we call windrows. We then take a team and a wagon with a hay frame and tall wooden standards at each end, drive the wagon down the windrow and fork the hay up on the wagon.

It takes someone on the wagon, who knows how to load hay real well without it sliding off. Since most of our hay is grown on the steep hillsides, you have to know what you're doing to stack it the right way, or else when you make a turn or hit a big gully, it will fall off. There is nothing worse than having a big load slide off, and then having to fork it on again. My granddad cusses only when something like this happens. He gets disgusted when things don't go right. If he is only a little disgusted, he will say "Damn it to hell." I've never heard him say, "God-damn," but he does say "shit" a lot, and sometimes will call a cow that is acting wild or a balky horse a "son-of-a-bitch." "Damn it to hell" is what he says whenever he gets a little disgusted, but he soon gets over it, and never gets so mad that he ever acts crazy.

We take wagon load after wagon load of hay to the barn. Our dairy barn is a big barn with a huge hayloft. It has a hay fork attached by ropes and pulleys with a long steel track running down the center of the loft up at the eve of the roof. The way we get the hay up in the loft is to drive the wagon under the big doors opening into the hayloft up at the top of the barn. The work-hand on the wagon sticks the hay fork down into a big section of hay, and then yells, "Take off."

I rode Dolly for years in pulling these big piles of hay up into the barn loft. She's our best horse for this. When I would say, "Giddup" and nudge her a little with my heels to her belly, she would hunch down and strain to pull the big fork of hay up into the loft. When it reaches the top, connects to the track and moves on down through the loft, one of the hands there hollers, "Ho!" when it's reached the point where it is to be dropped. I now have to go to the hayloft since I'm big enough to fork almost as much hay as a man.

74

When we're through unloading a load, we get to set in the shade of the barn and rest for a while. The hands come out of the loft wringing wet with sweat, and it takes them a while to catch their breath and roll a smoke. On a hot day, a hayloft is the hottest place there is. The sun beats down on the tin roof and you're wading around and forking and spreading the warm hay out over the loft and there is no air getting to you. And sometimes, wasps build nests in the loft, and you get stung and it's a relief when a wagon is unloaded and you can get down and get water and some air.

It's also a big relief when the first cutting of hay is in the barn. But you get a second and sometimes a third cutting later, so you're in hay off and on all summer. If there hasn't been enough rain early on, pasture and weed fields have to be cut for hay. A farmer always worries about whether he has enough hay to last a winter. When the loft gets full, we fill a section or two in the tobacco barn, and then make big haystacks out in a field if it has been seasonal and the fields keep growing.

During the busy planting time and hay time, we don't do much with the sheep. They've been sheared, and the ewes and their lambs wander around over the hills picking at grass and clover. In the heat of the day, they usually wander to the shade and stay there huffing and puffing to get their breath. My granddad rides Lady out to their shady spot nearly every day just to check on them. He'll sit there for a little while and just look. He can tell if anything is wrong with any of them, and they seem to know he's there to check, because they seldom ever spook and run away from him. We do worry about dogs getting in them and are always listening for that wild yelping from a pack day and night, but that doesn't happen too often.

We have to wean the lambs at the right time, which is usually when they are about four months old and about two-thirds grown. The ewes' bags have almost dried up by this time, and the lambs have to learn to graze on their own to fatten up for the market. When we drive them to the barn and separate the lambs from their mothers, it's a little sad, because they bleat and cry running around looking for each other. When the ewes are turned out into a field first, they run down over a hill bleating and looking for their own lambs. And the lambs do the same thing when they're turned out into another field. I never like weaning time, because I don't like to see anything sad. All the crying and bleating and looking for each other takes some getting used to. We can still hear them crying for each other in the night, but it settles down after a day or two. When we wean the lambs, I wonder what it must be like to have to leave your mother. I can't imagine what it's really like, and don't want to think about it. But we have to do a lot of hard things at times, and I know I'll have to not let the sad things bother me so much. My granddad goes right on and knows what he has to do without saying too much about it. He seems pretty rough at times, but I think he knows what's best for everything in the long run.

That doesn't mean I always go along with him on everything. Oh, I do what he tells me, like Crit, Sollie and the other hired hands do, but I sometimes wish we didn't have to do so many hard things so fast. During this time of year, it gets hard, because if you don't plant anything, you never have anything. And it's either go do it, or just drift along and never get ahead in life. I explained a lot about how we work and how you get a plant to grow and how to put up hay. The reason for explaining so much, I guess, is that I can't explain my life without telling about what we do. I suppose what you do is what your life is. Crit and Sollie go on steady each day and don't seem to have many dreams about something better or easier. They're happy every day just working and then taking their bucket of milk down the ridge after quitting time, and sitting out in the yard for a while until it gets dark.

I can't keep from thinking about maybe if I could be a baseball player and make a lot of money just playing and not working. I don't really know how good I might be at baseball, because I've never gotten to play in a real game yet. It's hard to imagine what my life might turn into, but it keeps me going to wonder about it.

# CHAPTER SIX

## THE CROPS ARE LAID BY

My life seems to have times when it eases up a little. And those times are when everything seems to be working together, and you feel good about what's to come. It's like when we lay the crops by.

At church when a farmer says, "I got mine laid by," you know he's not just bragging, but is very glad to have his work ease up a little. When the tobacco plants are out and beginning to grow and when the corn seeds have sprouted through the crust and the garden is beginning to bear, you can slack up some, but not too much until you lay the crops by. When the first cutting of hay has cured enough in the field and is then put up in the barn, you've got some of the hardest part over with. I know that city people don't always understand the way we country people talk.

But farm people have their own way of saying things, and I know exactly what they mean when they say something. When the crops are laid by, it means that you're almost through working with them until it's time to put them in the barn. So, it means you've done about all that you can do, and it's now up to the weather to make good crops, so you just hope, because there is not much you can do after that to help things along. When I say the weather, I also mean God, because he controls the weather, so you hope and pray.

Before the crops are laid by, you have to plow through the rows of tobacco and corn two or three times to help keep the ground loose and the weeds down. We use a five-shovel plow for tobacco and a three-shovel plow for corn, because corn ground doesn't have to be worked up so fine and nice. If you have a good single-line mare or horse, it makes plowing much easier and better. Some horses are good at it, and some are not. To get a horse to be a good single-liner, you have to know how to teach them and to handle them very gentle like. When you go to the tobacco patch to plow, you have to ride on some of the horses when pulling a plow through the rows, because some horses don't have a lot of sense or are too jumpy or ornery. Usually, a kid always rides the horse if this is the case, and it can get real tiresome all day long just sitting on a horse. You have to go very slow so the plow doesn't tear up the roots. When that happens, it's like tearing up a paycheck.

Bill is our best single-liner, and he knows how to plow tobacco. Dolly knows how to take a plow slowly through a row, but she gets fidgety at times. Single-line means that you only have to use one check line instead of two. You use the one line to help keep the horse in line and slowed down enough, and it's much easier than to have to hold two check lines and both plow handles at the same time. You and your horse must have an understanding, and some of them can learn your words real well and do what you tell them. A good horse knows that "gee" means to go right and "haw" to go left. "Whoa" and "giddup" and "ho down" to slow them down are some of the other words they can learn. The best ones even know that how you say a word tells them what to do. If you say "gee" real loud like, they turn right a whole lot. Once in a while, you have a plow horse so good they don't need any line at all, because they know exactly what you want them to do when they learn what you're saying. Whenever it's time to buy or trade a horse, every farmer wants to know if it is a single-liner. Lady is very smart when she wants to be. You can be on her bringing in sheep and she really knows when one drifts off and will go after it sometimes without you even nudging her. Horses are like the kids in school. Some of them are smart, and some of them are not very smart.

I used to have to ride a horse sometimes when two or three of us were plowing, and we didn't have all our horses as a single-liner. I never liked it much, because the sweat would build up and soak my pants and they would get wet and stiff and the white-lather sweat would stink. I'd sit up there all day and think about things, and sometimes get sleepy-like and let the horse drift over too close and step on a plant, and my granddad would get a little disgusted.

Now I chop out and hoe, and will probably be plowing next year, because my arms are not strong enough yet to hold the plow steady and close to a plant. When the five-shovel plow goes through a row, some of us have to follow behind and chop out the remaining weeds and hoe the dirt around each plant real smooth. If it has been rainy and the grass and weeds have grown too fast, it takes many days of chopping to get everything clean and pretty again. You don't have to be as particular in chopping out corn, because corn grows fast and will usually overtake the weeds. I used to chop out one row of tobacco at a time, while a hand chopped out two rows at a time. Kids are kind of pushed into working up to doing what a man can do as soon as they can.

When it gets long and hot out in a July field, we get to take a little break at the end of a row. Sitting under a shade tree and telling stories while the horse blows or eats some grass is kind of restful. We always keep a water jug in the shade unless there is a spring nearby. The cool water from a good spring tastes mighty good when you're hot. We keep an old tin can at these springs to drink from, and it's much better than the warm water from a jug. I like to sit there and listen to the cool water trickle out of the ground. It makes a little peaceful sound. And it cools your face and arms to splash some of it on you.

When the last plowing is finished and all the weeds are chopped out and the first cutting of hay is in, it's a good feeling. It's like you don't have to get so much done all at once.

We get to take a day or two off for the Fourth of July. They have a celebration in town and a little carnival with some rides and food and ice cream and all kinds of cold drinks with ice. They have shows and games like knocking bottles down with a baseball or throwing rings over certain dolls or things to win prizes. And they have rides that are run by motors and music playing, and it's exciting. I used to ride the merry-go-round when I was little. Of course, now I ride a real horse nearly every day, so the merry-go-round is for littler kids. I ride the big Ferris wheel now by myself or with a friend. You go way up and can see all over town, and it's just a little scary, but gives you a big thrill to be up that high.

My granddad mainly stays at the cattle and horse shows. He can just sit there hour after hour and talk to other farmers about this horse or that cow. They laugh and are restful sitting in the shade under the grandstand roof. He likes to see good stock and studies them so he can grow the best stock he can. The games and the rides and the ice cream and everything is what I like to do. I don't just want to sit and watch the cattle shows. I see enough cattle every day.

Last year, my granddad told me he was giving me a dairy calf for my own. I think he wanted me to learn how you can make money. Many of the older boys in high school raise a little tobacco crop and some own a few cattle or sheep of their own. Most of them stay in farming when they get tired of school, and many of them get married and start out on their own when they're 17 or 18. So they have to know how to make a living.

He gave me this little Holstein heifer calf, and it was mostly white with a few black patches, and it was real pretty. I always paid special attention to it, because it was mine. Well, we were in the 4-H Club at school. It was the only club I ever belonged to. The county agent would come out every month or two and talk to us about farming and having projects of our own. He wanted us to show our calves and lambs on the Fourth of July. So I got my calf all trimmed and clean and trained to lead with a halter and rope, and we took it to the show. That morning, I showed it and won second place and a red ribbon. The boys always tied the ribbons to the halter so people would know what happened. After the show, we left our calves tied up under a tent, so we could go back to the rides and games for a while. When we got ready to leave, I went to my calf and she had eaten the red ribbon and left only a little bit at the end. It was all wet, and I was a little disappointed, because I had nothing to show for it.

Also during the Fourth of July, you can buy firecrackers, and some of them are big and real powerful. My mother is always scared, but Henry and I try to get some and take them to the barn lot and set them off. The best way is to put one in a big cow pile, light it and watch the manure scatter all over and even splatter way high up on the barn and silo. You have to run away fast after lighting it, because if you don't, it will splatter the wet manure all over you.

My heifer calf will soon be ready to breed, and then I will have two head of stock. By the time I'm 17 or 18, I'll have three or four head. It seems like you pay more attention when you own something, so you actually take more interest in everything when it means more to you. When I was about 7, my granddad bought me a goat. He made a little harness so it could pull my wagon. Goats can get contrary, though, and are always into everything. We finally sold the goat for $4 at the stockyards, and I had my first money ever that somebody didn't give to me.

As I said, some of the high school boys have several head of cattle and raise a little tobacco crop of their own. They also work for the neighbors some and can pick up a few dollars that way. Most of them buy a car as soon as they get their license, and decorate it with lights and loud mufflers and tie a coon tail on the front or on the radio aerial. They all drive pretty fast, and my mother never wants me to ride with them. But I want to begin making more money so I can get a car when I get my license. My granddad says that I don't need a car. He once said that you can't waste your money on a car if you ever think about going on and getting an education. He didn't say that I was going on, but it did get me to thinking more about it. That's the way he is. Whenever he says something, it gets you to thinking more about what he said, and I doubt if he'll let me buy a car while I'm in high school. He may be right, but it gets lonely being stuck out here on the farm all the time. The boys who have cars are always trying to come up with enough gas money. If it takes all you can make to keep a car on the road, then I can see how you couldn't come up with enough for an education.

When the Fourth of July is over, we have to get serious again about work. With the crops laid by, we don't have to do much with them but watch them grow. If it is seasonable and has rained enough, then the second cutting of hay begins to come on. It seems like we're always in hay off and on all summer. If my granddad thinks we might not have enough hay or if it hasn't grown too good, then we have to cut and put up pasture fields.

Everything depends on the weather. I keep telling you about the weather, but there's no way to get around it. Some years, it gets too dry in the summer. You see the tobacco just sit there in the field and turn yellow, and there is not much you can do about it. Sometimes it rains so hard with gully-washers that it washes the dirt away and you lose some of the plants. The worst fear, though, is a bad hailstorm. Hail will shred the tender tobacco leaves or break them from the stalk. If this happens, it can take away most of a year's work, and a farmer can almost be wiped out. If you've cut a big field of hay, and it starts to rain and won't stop, the hay can rot in the field. So each morning at milking time, Crit might say, "What's the weather gonna bring today?" If it's threatening rain, then you don't want to go and mow a big field of good alfalfa. If it has been a dry spell and the crust around the tobacco has dried and hardened, then you may want to go back and plow it again and stir up the earth to give it some life.

Most farmers who go to church believe that the weather is tied in with God. Whenever we're in a drought, we never actually pray out loud for God to send rain, but some farmers or their wives pray for rain at the blessing during meal time. I've heard them pray something like this: "Dear God, as you know we need rain for the crops. And if it's your will to send rain, then we would be mighty thankful. Whatever your will is we will abide, and we give thanks for this food and all your blessings. Amen." I wonder why we can't understand God's will better, because it seems like we never know why he keeps the rain from us when we're doing the best we can.

One dry summer we had a bad drought, and the grasshoppers came in real bad. They went into the tobacco patches in droves and began eating up the leaves. We had to go out and take pieces of tin and bang it with a stick and try to drive and scare them out. We walked through each row and banged and hollered, and the grasshoppers would scurry out. It seems like if it's not one thing with the weather, it's something else. During a real dry spell, the creeks and springs dry up and the ponds get low. When this happens, I have to drive our cows to a spring still running or pond still holding some water so they can drink.

One hot summer, it got very dry. The tobacco looked like it was dead and the hay fields and pastures turned brown and the dust blew and the trees looked limp. All our neighbors were worried. And then it started raining gentle like just when things looked hopeless. You could almost see the grass come alive as the dust was washed off, and the tobacco and corn perked up. When this rain started coming, the word got out that there would be a church service. I never remember anything like this before, a sudden church service. We went that night, and it was because the people were so thankful and happy for the rain. We sat there in the cool, fresh evening, with the windows open and the air moist and clean. And the preacher said to sing, "There Shall Be Showers of Blessings," and everybody really started singing more than they usually did. The second verse meant the most. It went, "There shall be showers of blessings, Precious reviving again; Over the hills and the valleys, sound of abundance of rain. Showers of blessings, Showers of blessings we need; Mercy drops round us are falling, But for the showers we plead." And we sang it two or three times, and I noticed that some of the old farmers, who usually never sang, were joining in and you could hear their deep, rough voices over the women. And some of the women looked like they might cry, and the preacher said that we don't always know about God's plan, but that he always takes care of us.

I don't know whether to worry over God's plan or not. Some of our preachers in the past have said that picture shows are sinful. They have said that Saturday night is the Devil's night. If I get to go to the picture show on Saturday, I have tried to believe that the Devil is not there. One of my great aunts got on me a little about certain comic books like Superman and Captain Marvel, and some of my relatives believe it is sinful to play baseball on Sunday. They also think you should never do any work on Sunday, but we have to milk, feed and clean out the manure every Sunday like we do every other day. We've also had to work a few times on Sunday, when we had too much hay on the ground and it was threatening rain, or too much tobacco cut and it was getting sunburned in the field.

Once there was a question about whether the women should stay home from church and cook a big dinner for the preacher when he came. Some people thought a woman should go to church whether the preacher was coming or not. But some of the women said they could not do the preacher right if they couldn't stay home and get a good big dinner ready. The preacher goes to a different home each Sunday. When he comes to ours, we clean up the house real good, and sometimes I have to help. I've never liked doing women's work around the house. My mother always stays home and tries to put on a big dinner when the preacher comes. She uses the dining room and has the table set real special with our good dishes. The preachers always act like they like a big dinner, because of the way they eat after a fiery sermon. I guess it makes them real hungry. We've had preachers who believe that smoking is sinful, especially women smoking cigarettes. Of course, the question came up that it was okay to raise tobacco, but not to smoke it. So some of the things about being good all the time are confusing.

I used to want to sneak a cigarette, but not now. I know that if I want to be a player on the Morgan Raiders team, I can't smoke, because I won't have as much wind. And I don't want to drink beer like some of the high school boys do. They get together on Saturday nights, buy beer from a bootlegger, get drunk and throw up. I think my granddad has drunk a little, but he never shows it. One time, we had some uncles come, and I heard him ask them if they would like a drink of moonshine, and he took them up in the attic over the kitchen, where I think he had a jar hid. He's never shown any other signs of keeping whiskey or anything in the house.

He's mostly interested in his sheep and the crops. In the early summer, he's interested in getting the lambs fat for market. I heard him say that the people up in New York sure like their spring lamb. He always wants to have some of our lambs ready for market in late spring. We bring them to the barn, put 20 or so in each stall, and he studies them and tries to pick out the fattest ones. He moves slowly through them and rubs his fingers along their backbone trying to feel the fat. Their wool has grown to an inch or more, so you can't tell how fat they are by just looking. He lifts some of them up and has us lift them up and try to guess the weight. We put a few on the scales to get the actual weight. It's like a little guessing game, and it makes the work more interesting whenever we can make a game out of it. He likes to sell a lamb around 80 pounds.

If a lamb brings 20 cents a pound, then a 90-pound lamb brings four dollars more than a 70-pound lamb. So it's very important to get the most to make ends meet. Before the truck comes to take them to market, he won't let them drink water overnight. Then, when we're about to load them early the next morning, we let them go to the pond and hope they fill up and drink a pound or two of water to get an extra few cents at the sale. He really likes having a truckload of good lambs ready. Later in the summer, we take the rest of the lambs to market, and by that time, it's almost breeding season again.

July is a slack month with crops, but there is fence to build or fix, barns and roofs to paint or fix, pastures to mow, rocks to haul and many other little things that back up. So we keep at it. As the hot summer days move on, we aren't so rushed, but there is always something that needs to be done. I've never liked having to wander around over the hills and cut cockle-burrs and thistles, which we do a few days in the summer. If we don't, the burrs get all matted in the sheep's wool, and hang on their bellies, and my granddad never wants to see one of his sheep looking like that.

Around the middle of July, the wild blackberries get ripe out in the fields, and we take a day or two to pick them. My mother cans quart after quart of the ripe berries and makes pint after pint of blackberry jam. She makes big blackberry cobblers, and there is nothing like a fresh cobbler during blackberry-picking time. Picking them is another job that is not so good, but it doesn't last too long. It always seems so hot in a blackberry patch, and you have to be careful with the thorns and look for big snakes and not stand too long in one spot so that the chiggers get on you. For some reason, black snakes and spreading vipers seem to like staying in the thick of a briar patch. Maybe it's because they have more protection there.

Picking berries is like everything else we do. You have to learn how to do it fast, or you'd never get anywhere. I take a gallon bucket, loop my belt through the handle and have it handy in front of me so I can pick with both hands. After a day of picking and even at dinnertime, I have to wash up good to get the chiggers off.

In the summer, I take a bath nearly every day. At noon, I pump a wash tub about one-third full out at the cistern to let it warm in the afternoon sun. At night, I take the tub to the smokehouse and scrub down. It is much easier to take a bath in the summer than in the winter, when I have to set a teakettle on the stove, bring the tub into the kitchen after supper and wash off. In the winter, I take a bath once or twice a week unless I get a lot of manure on me at the barn. I can't wait to get to Morgan High School and practice basketball every day the last period and then get to take a shower in their dressing room. And I can't wait to go down in the basement in that dressing room, put on that shiny gold uniform and run out on the floor and listen to all the cheering. Sometimes when I'm doing something like picking blackberries, I cheer up thinking about the good shower over in their dressing room.

As I've said, my mother stays in the house and she and my sister take care of everything there. She doesn't go out and help in the fields. Most farm women stay around the house. A few women do like to get out of the house, and a few work in the fields at times or help milk in the evenings or work the garden. The men and boys mostly do everything outside and the women and girls do everything inside. Men don't hang around the house and almost never do anything in the kitchen. Even on rainy or cold days or during a slack time, the men and boys hang around the barns. The men sit around the house a little on Sunday afternoons in their Sunday clothes, but I can tell that my granddad gets anxious to change his clothes, and just go out to the barn and wander around looking at the stock. Sunday clothes even make me feel like I'm not really free.

My mother takes care of all the cooking and all the clothes. In the summer, she cans everything she can from the garden, because we never buy anything unless we have to, and of course, we always have to be very careful about our money. She cans corn, beets, green beans, peas, cucumber relish with peppers and onions, tomatoes, tomato juice, tomato chili sauce, pickles, berries, peaches, and cherries. After hog-killing time, she cooks sausage, ribs and backbones and cans some of them in big jars. She does the washing on a Monday, and does a lot of sewing and patching. All the rough work outside is hard on clothes so she has to keep patching the overalls over and over until they completely wear out.

We men have to do a few things around the house, but we never want to be around there too much. We build a fire under the big wash kettle on Monday mornings so she can have hot water to wash the clothes. And during the summer, we kill, scald and pluck a couple of frying chickens and pick some beans, onions, corn, tomatoes and other things for the day's dinner. And of course in the winter, I have to make sure we always have enough heating wood and buckets of coal stacked up on the back porch. But we're anxious to get to the fields, and the only time during the day that we want to go in the house is at dinnertime.

Some farm women use a big dinner bell in the back yard to let the men know when it's dinnertime, but we always eat dinner at 12 o'clock. At dinnertime, we take the work horses to water, put them in their stalls, give them a few ears of corn and head for the house. They get to start eating their dinner before we do, but it's like that. You take care of everything else and then take care of yourself. After a long, hot morning in the hay field or tobacco patch, we wash up a little at the cistern, and then head for the big table on the back porch. It feels mighty good to sit down in the cool and start passing the biscuits and the gravy and the fried chicken and corn, beans, mashed potatoes and everything. And we're so full afterwards, and go out and lie on the grass under the poplar shade tree in the back yard and feel so drowsy and lazy. But my granddad soon says, "Go get the horses," and we head back to the field. He never believes in sitting down on the job for very long.

After the war, everything got much better. Everybody was very worried during the war, and many of the men were off fighting, and you never knew when the government would come and tell you they were missing in action or killed in action. So it was hard to keep from worrying. The war also made it real hard for farmers, because most all of the younger men were gone, so the hard work was left to the older men and the kids. Many of the farm women began to work more and more out in the fields whether they wanted to or not, because there was no one else to do it.

When the war started, everybody was afraid, and nobody actually wanted to go to the war and maybe be killed. The times were sad, and people didn't know what to do in a way. The government had to draft almost all the younger men in the Army or Navy, but certain ones did not have to go. If you had bad feet or eyes, you couldn't march or shoot, so the weaker ones didn't have to go. And some farmers did not have to go, because the country still had to have food to feed everybody. So the draft board said that if a young farmer was raising a lot of crops, they didn't have to go to war.

One of my uncles, who lived and worked in town, talked about it a lot and worried, and then he and my aunt and my little cousin, Sue, decided to move in with us. Since he could prove he was farming, the draft board wouldn't take him. In the early spring, they moved into two of our rooms at the side of the house and he started farming with us. I was nine at the time, but I was glad to have them at our place, because it was more fun for me. With them and little Sue there, our house was much different. I worked with my uncle and was with him nearly every day in the field. He talked a lot about the war, and it bothered and worried him so much that most of his friends had to go off to war and he didn't have to go.

He smoked Camel cigarettes and my aunt smoked Chesterfields. Many town women smoked, and Chesterfields were more like a cigarette for women. They said Camels were stronger and more of a man cigarette. Town people usually smoked regular cigarettes, and farm people mostly smoked Bull Durham or Buffalo, which you have to roll in a cigarette paper every time you want a smoke. Regular cigarettes cost more than sack tobacco, and town people usually have more money than country people so they don't have to roll their own. Some of the poorer tenant farmers crumble up dried tobacco leaves at the barn, tear off a piece of paper sack and make smoking that doesn't cost them anything.

I started to wonder how they all tasted and wanted to be big like high school boys and like my uncle. My mother and granddad never wanted me to do anything like older boys, but even when I was little, I always wanted to show everybody I could do big things. I began to figure out how I could smoke one of their cigarettes. Whenever they would light up, I would try to smell the difference between a Camel and a Chesterfield. A Chesterfield seemed more sweet-like, so I guess that's why it is more of a cigarette for women.

One time a year or so ago, I thought I would be big and was out at the barn with some of the hands, and my granddad wasn't there. I knew some of the boys at school had smoked dried corn silks, so I decided to smoke a corn-silk cigarette and rolled one in an old piece of paper sack. Corn silks grow out the end of an ear of corn and turn brown when they dry up. I rolled it and lit up and acted like I could do whatever the men could do. There was really no taste to the corn silks, but the blue smoke rolled out and I was puffing away when my granddad came around the corner of the milk house. It shocked me and scared me. He walked right up to me, took the cigarette and tore it apart to see what it was. He then stomped it on the ground and walked away. I was so scared. He didn't say anything, but just looked at me real strong. That was the way it went, because I always knew what I should not ever do. So I never thought about smoking for a while, because I knew it would mean trouble if he or my mother ever found out.

But I kept wondering what a Camel would taste like, so one late afternoon when I had to go after the cows, I sneaked a couple of cigarettes out of my uncle's and aunt's packs when they weren't looking. I took a couple of kitchen matches, and when I got over the hill in back of the house, I lit one up. I blew the blue smoke out like they do. It didn't taste like I thought it would. I flipped the ashes off with my finger like my uncle does, and as I walked along puffing and flipping, I did feel like I was like the older men. I don't know why I think that the older boys and men will like me better if I can do everything they can do. But I keep trying to do everything I have to do so they will like me more all the time.

The war bothered my uncle so much that he decided to tell the draft board to take him and that he was quitting farming. Most young farmers finally went into the army, but a few tried to stay out, and people at church would say they were cowards and afraid. Everyone was afraid, but my granddad said President Roosevelt said that we should not get too scared, but just go on and be brave and fight and win. My granddad never acted like he was afraid of anything, and it made me feel easier too. My uncle went into the Army and was sent to Germany to fight against Hitler and the bad Germans. The Germans wore those helmets that curved down over their necks, and it made them look even more scary. The Japs were scary too. They hid in palm trees and were called snipers and would sneak to shoot you. They used dive-bombers to sink our ships, and we couldn't understand why they would just kill themselves so they could kill Americans.

When I was little and the war was going on, we used to play war with sticks as our guns. We also talked about whether we would rather kill Japs or Germans. My older friend Henry knew a lot about the war, and he would tell me about fighter planes like the P-39 Mustangs and the P-41s. We sometimes talked about how we wished we were old enough to go and fight. We would say that we would be brave and not be afraid, but then when I was alone, I'd get thinking about it and get scared again.

My mother and my aunt Fay worried almost all the time. Every so often, a letter would come from my uncle, and he would tell them to not worry. He told about taking over towns in Germany, and about not having much food or having nothing but flour for pancakes with no syrup. People would read and reread these letters, and it would usually cheer everyone up for a little while. The best way to be cheered up was to talk about what everybody would do after the war. My aunt would begin being happy when she could talk about what they would do when my uncle came home. But it was mostly just waiting and hoping and praying. People seem different when they are just waiting and hoping. We couldn't talk about the war all the time, because it would keep us worrying all the time. Although people were not very happy and didn't get to go places or have much fun, it seemed like most everybody never gave up hope.

My granddad worked to collect scrap metal for the war, and he had meetings in town to work on things that people at home could do to support our boys. Whenever he started something, he didn't stop until it was done. He would laugh a little when he heard on the radio that General Eisenhower or General MacArthur had won another battle and moved on toward Germany or Japan. He never criticized our government like some people did.

The stores came out with a little flag that you hung in a front window. It had a red trim around a white part, and it had a gold fringe around the sides. If you had a son or grandson off at the war, then you bought a flag that had one blue star in the middle. If you had two, then you bought a flag with two blue stars. Raymond Smith, a blacksmith up past the Locust Grove store, had six sons in the war, and they had to buy two flags with three stars each to hang in their window. Everybody then knew which houses had sons at war.

I had about seven or eight uncles or cousins off in the war, and only two of them did not come back. Then you bought a flag with a gold star, which meant that they had been killed. Every time we would go past a neighbor or anyone who had a gold star in the window, I could tell that my granddad was thinking about it all so much and about his son and son-in-law and all his nephews.

When the boys finally came home, it was a glad and happy time. It was like starting everything over. It was like starting a new crop year in the early spring when the plant beds were sowed. It was like lambing time in January. It was like planting the corn and bean and melon seeds when the earth warmed in May. Every time we start a new crop year or have lambs come on, it is always a hopeful time. We never knew what the year would bring, but it seemed the farmers who hope the most, do the best.

When the boys began coming home, we had dinners and get-togethers to welcome them back. When things settled down after Truman dropped the atomic bomb on Japan, everybody just wanted to get started all over again. I was young during the war and didn't understand why we had to fight, but knew that Hitler and Mussolini and Tojo were real bad people. It bothered me to see my mother and aunt and everybody worried so. I didn't think too much about myself and the war, but now they are talking about Communism building up, and my granddad says that Stalin is about as bad as Hitler. I do think once in a while about if I will have to go fight. We've always had war, so you have to get used to it. My older great uncles used to talk some about World War I, and I know what World War II was like. My granddad told us a little about his dad who was in the Civil War. And now they say we'll be fighting in Korea next, so I guess I'll have to fight someday, but it kind of scares me when I think about getting killed in a far off place.

I could tell you a lot more about the big war, but that's over. My life is moving right along, and I was telling how we laid the crops by in the middle of the summer and then started jumping all over the place. As I get older, that's kind of the way it is, jumping all over the place.

When the crops are laid by and growing through the summer, a farmer has to catch up on many other things. Even if everything is growing and looks good, there are rocks to haul off the fields, bushes to cut and always mowing to keep the weeds down in the pastures. One day last summer, my granddad said, "Let's all go to the stock yards." Of course, he always goes when he is selling lambs or a cow or two, but we have to stay and work. So the hands and I got to go that afternoon. It was pretty exciting for us, because we got to drink cold soft drinks and eat one or two candy bars, and we didn't have to work. The farmers sit around the selling pit and listen to the auctioneer sing away as the stock is brought in. Sometimes a farmer is real happy if his stock brings a good price, but sometimes it doesn't. There's a lot of talking and carrying on, and you get to see other people for a change. I think my granddad just wanted to give us a little treat that day. He's never much for just taking off any, so he surprised us. He is kind of like that. He is mostly the same day after day and very steady with everything, but every once in a while, he does a little something for you. It isn't very often, but you get to know that he thinks about you once in a while.

July is a fresher month than August. It's not as fresh and green as June is when everything is growing so fast you can't keep up with it. But as the month wears down, you can see that the dry August days are about to come as it gets dustier and hazier. And the heat stays with you longer and sticks to you. The cool, fresh dew in the mornings is usually burnt off way before dinnertime. And it's like everything is beginning to slowly fade into a yellowish-brown wasted look. The bright green grass and the clearer blue skies of early July slowly take on a coat of dusty haze. The sheep lie longer each day in their shady spots. The milk cows work harder to find fresh sprigs of grass and their milk begins to drop off. The dogs get lazier and the horses wear down. As the early morning dew and the mid-day sweat keep our work shoes wet and soft, the longer hot days dry them out. Early every morning, I sit at the kitchen door by the back porch, where we always leave our work shoes. Well into the summer, they're cracked and hardened and rub against your feet when they're pulled on. It takes a while each day for them to soften again. And our faces and arms get as brown as the sorrel coat of our riding mare. Since I never wear a shirt, my back gets so brown and tough that it looks like what my uncle said, "A piece of whit leather."

We change along with the seasons. My back is light and tender in the spring, but now it turns the sun away. My hands become hard and callused by this time of year. A cut or scrape or splinter doesn't sting as much, because my hands have been toughened after days of hauling rocks and chopping weeds and forking hay. The points of the thorns and briars are blunted against the leathery skin. My granddad will grab hold of anything, and he expects me to do the same. When the time is right, he says you have to take hold. It will soon be tobacco-housing time, and I'll be cutting it like a man this year. I want to show them I can take hold and am changing into a man.

# CHAPTER SEVEN

## IT WILL SOON BE TOPPING TIME

Sometimes I wish I could grow as fast as a tobacco plant so I'd be a man sooner. A tobacco plant can grow up to five or six feet in about three months. I don't want it to come that fast, and I'll have to not get too anxious about it. That day will come, I guess, when people will think I'm big enough and old enough to do everything.

A tobacco patch looks mighty good when the stalks grow up to over a man's belt. If it's a seasonable year, the tobacco stays green, and the greener it stays, the bigger it grows. If the ground stays moist from regular rains, the leaves turn to a rich dark green, and it grows up to a man's shoulders or more. In early August the plants begin to bloom. They shoot out a tall pink-white flower at the top about the size of a big fist, and it looks like a field of pretty flowers all in a row. When the blooms reach to about the top of your head, it's time to top the plants.

We go through each row and twist and break each bloom off at about a foot below the top of the bloom. When it is snapped off, the juice flows and your hands become caked with sticky black gum. By dinnertime, your hands are coated with the thick gum, and if you have cracks on your hands, it makes them sting and burn. When the topping is done, the plants begin to spread and the leaves thicken and widen. You can see the dark green leaves begin to take on a yellow tint. After topping time, it's only a few weeks until the tobacco is ripe and ready for cutting and housing. And this is what you worked for to finally get a crop in the barn.

My granddad doesn't always stay in the field with us doing everything. He is getting older and his joints hurt and his hands and fingers are getting stiffer all the time. If he has to squeeze a pitchfork or a hoe-handle all day long, he can't get his fingers straightened out at night. He rides out each day on Lady and checks on the cattle and sheep and the fences and everything. He also stops by from time to time to see how we are getting along at whatever we're doing.

I spend most of my time with our tenants. I've told you mostly about Crit and Sollie, because they are our tenants now and have been with us for a couple of years. But we've had many different tenants through the years. We've had John, Raymond, Jim, Chester, Isaac, Walter and others on our place. Tenants move around quite a lot. They stay with you for a year or two, and then seem to get restless or think they can get something better and move on. Whenever one comes to our farm, they know they have to work every day and not stop, because they've heard about my granddad's reputation. They never agree to be our tenant if they aren't willing to work.

Usually, in late winter, a tenant who wants to move to a new place begins talking to people at the store to spread the word that he wants to move. When my granddad is interested in a different tenant, he will tell him exactly what he will do and how the money part will work out. He might tell the new tenant that he can raise two acres of tobacco of his own and milk the cows, put up the hay and get one-half of the milk check. The tenant would also get one-half of the money from the two acres of his tobacco crop. When the tenants aren't working in their own crop, they work every day for my granddad at three dollars a day. And they get to live in one of the little houses back on the ridge. They only have to buy a little food they don't raise in their garden and a few clothes now and then, so they make enough to live on, but nothing extra. Whenever my granddad agrees to take on a new tenant, they never write anything down on paper. They just agree right there and go on for the year.

Some of our tenants came from out of the mountains in lower Kentucky, hoping to better themselves. They had their ways that were different from us. They knew a lot about hunting and trapping and a lot of things about nature. They talked different and would use mostly the same words we used, but say them different. They would not say "right" and "night" and "light" like we do, but say it more slow and drawn out to where it sounded like some other word. Most of them had a dog or two, a few chickens and that was about it. Some of them can afford a battery radio like we had before electricity, and they love to play music on it. Mountain music with fiddles, banjos and mandolins keeps them in a good mood, and they whistle, yodel and sing some out in the fields. They get to town maybe three or four times a year, and this is big to them.

Most tenant families don't go to church. Every once in a while, the preacher tries to get them to come to save their souls, and they might go for a time or two, but soon give it up. I think their clothes

94

are the main reason, and some of them don't have any Sunday clothes whatsoever. Many of them can't read or only a little, and when the preacher says to open your Bibles, or we are studying from the Sunday school lesson book, they don't know what to do. They just feel uneasy sitting there.

Most of the tenants have a lot of kids, and most of the kids also go to the field to work, so I'm with these kids most every day. I always have on better clothes and shoes than they do, but I don't want to act like I am rich or anything around them, so I try to act like them, because I fit in better that way. Not many of them really like school, so we don't mention things in books or papers very much. We don't think we're better than the tenant farmers, but maybe in a way we do, because my granddad says most of them never want to get very far ahead or do anything different.

When I go to town, I sometimes think the town boys think they're better than me. They even talk different from me, and if I am ever around kids from the big city, they look even better and talk like they've learned everything in school. It's like I'm better than the tenant kids, but not as good as town kids or city kids.

But it's funny when we have some relatives come from the city and bring their kids. Then I can show them a lot. I'll go bridle up a horse and jump on, and they are almost scared to get close. Or I'll take them to watch us milk and maybe squirt some milk at their feet, and they don't even want to touch a cow let alone its tits. And their parents are usually afraid that their city kids will get hurt or eaten by a hog or something, and it's really funny how they are. But I get to show them how much I can do and not be afraid at all.

When I was going on 11, we had the Carter family with eight kids move in as tenants. They were pretty ignorant and dirtier than most. But with a big family, they could do a lot of work. Not only did Isaac come to milk and then go to the field each morning, but he brought along four of his kids, including Norma and Lucy, who were about 15 and 16. I overheard my mother tell my granddad that she was worried they might try to mess with me about sex. I already knew all about how things breed, because I saw it everyday. But I wasn't interested in girls or touching them or anything like that. I do know at school, some of the eighth grade boys try to get a couple of the girls in the coatroom so they can feel them, and I've heard some of the boys who go on over to high school talk about who is putting out.

But anyway, Lucy was smart and kind of led the family. She did all the figuring with my granddad at pay time. But the Carter family was always having different relatives or people come to their place, and a boy of about 18 came and stayed for a while. Lucy told me that he began sneaking out with Norma and going to the hayloft and sticking her, and I knew what she meant.

Most of the tenants are pretty good people and do what they're told. My mother doesn't want any of them talking dirty around me and my granddad doesn't either, so they don't. They joke some about farting and shitting, and once in a while they say something about getting a little last night, and laugh about it, but that's about it.

If a tenant family is real good at work and raising crops, they usually move on after a year or two. They get a job on the railroad or highway department and make a little more money for their families than they can at farming. It beats just barely making it from year to year.

After the tobacco is topped, most of the hay has been put up, although there might be a third cutting later in early fall. It's a slack time, but we just don't do nothing. The tobacco barns have to be ready for housing, and if things are in pretty good shape, there's winter wood to cut. We try to wait until later in cooler weather to cut wood, because it is such a hot job chopping with an ax and using a cross-cut saw in the heat of summer. The sheep take almost no care during this last real hot month of summer except checking on them every day or two. It's easy, because they've gathered at their shady spots, and my granddad rides out and just looks at them for a spell and can tell if there's anything wrong. Sometimes he wants me to go along in case we have to look for strays, and I then have to go down over a hill in the thick bushes and look for a lost one. If we're going to change pastures, I have to help round them up. Sometimes they get contrary and don't want to drive, especially on real hot days, and I have to run up and down hills and cut off those heading for the hollows. It can get pretty rough with all the running over the hills. Crit and Sollie never like to run that much at all, so I'm the one my granddad depends on to do the running after them. I don't like it too

96

much either, but try to think it will help me in basketball when I get to play on the big team in high school.

One day, my granddad told me to get the horses and wagon so we could go kill a lamb and bring it in to eat. In the summer, you get tired of eating fried chicken everyday, but that's the kind of meat we mostly have. You have to have meat every meal to give you enough strength to do the work. Most of the cured hog meat, hams, bacon and shoulders have been used up, so it's chicken, and once in a while we kill a mess of squirrels for a change. The tenants never have a lot of meat, but get the grease from a little cured side meat for gravy and this gives them strength. They also buy a lot of baloney at Perry's store or from Charlie's huckster truck, but my granddad says baloney isn't fit to eat. In the winter, we kill a beef and eat on it during the cold times when it will keep. Or sometimes three or four farmers go together and kill a beef and then split it up and eat on it before it spoils.

We took the wagon to the field, and my granddad pointed out a lamb he wanted me to catch. When I caught it, he came up, straddled it, took a rock and hit it real hard in the head to stun it. He then took out his pocketknife, slit the lamb's throat and held its head so all the blood would shoot out. You have to let an animal bleed real good when it's killed for meat.

It's always hard for me to be around all that blood and to watch something die. The blood is almost hot when it comes out, and it makes you get a little dizzy at first. But my granddad does it like it doesn't amount to much. He likes his sheep and is always doing the best for them, so I wonder how he never let killing one of them bother him, but maybe it does. I guess he does hard things so much, and maybe if you keep doing hard things, it gets easier to do them, but I don't know yet.

When the lamb had bled out, we tied its hind legs up to a tree branch. His hands and his knife were bloody by this time, and I had some on me, but we went on. He began cutting through the soft woolly skin around each leg and made slits through the skin down its stomach and around its throat. Then I had to grab one side of the skin and he had the other, and we pulled it all the way down. I could hear a little ripping sound as we pulled it clear off, and then he cut its head off. Seeing the head lying there on the ground made me think about a lot of things. I didn't have time to think much, because he then cut all the way down through its stomach and the guts fell out.

I'd watched him kill a lamb and other things many times before, but I am now old enough to help out. He told me to drag the guts and the head down over the hill and throw them in a hollow for the buzzards. In about a day, we'd see buzzards circling. I picked up the guts and the head and tried not to smell or look. I kept on not looking at what I was dragging and kept trying to breathe fresh air, but by this time I had blood on my arms and overalls and couldn't get away from the smell. When I got back to him, he told me to take a bucket and go get some water from a nearby pond. I went to the pond and washed off my hands and arms as best I could, and took a bucket of water back. He splashed the little pink carcass off with the water to cool it down some, and then we loaded it on the wagon and headed for the house.

We'd now have lamb to eat for a few days. My mother would fry up the chops, and make leg roasts, which would be better than eating chicken every day. When I ate it, I sure tried not to think about the head lying there on the ground. I guess it's no different from eating chickens or beef or rabbits, but a lot of people won't eat lamb for some reason, especially town people, because they say little lambs are too cute. They are, and they never try to hurt anything like a cow that kicks or a horse that might buck you off. But you have to not think about everything so much, but sometimes you can't keep from thinking about living the way we do.

I hate to tell you this in a way, but last year I killed a skunk for no good reason. One day, when I went to the mailbox at dinnertime, I looked in our garage and saw a skunk wandering around in there. Farm people always put their garage down by the road and not up by the house. In the old days when cars first came out, people thought cars might blow up with all that gasoline in them, so they kept them away from the house.

When I saw the skunk, I ran to the house and got my 22 rifle. My granddad had given me this single-shot rifle, because every boy has to learn how to shoot, and your first gun is like a sign that you have almost grown up. I ran back to the garage hoping that the skunk was still there, and without giving it the first thought, fired and killed it with one shot. Well, it fell over on its back, and began kicking and squirming and then let loose with its piss spray that went all over the garage. The stink took my breath completely away, and it was so bad that I had to run a little ways away. Then I stopped and thought about it lying there and kicking. It made me feel real bad, but then I tried to feel better, because we killed rats and groundhogs and stray dogs and many other things all the time. I couldn't get out of my mind the way it lay there on its back kicking and dying. It would have gone away back to its hole and not bothered anything, so I thought that I would never kill anything again unless I had to.

Certain things you do like what I've been telling about killing, settle on your mind more than most other things we do everyday. One thing on my mind more and more is getting saved at church. Sometimes I think God is actually talking to me about getting saved, but, of course, it's never anything that I can actually hear.

In late August, we have a revival at our church, and I did have to go to Bible School during the day along with it when I was younger. But we have the revival at this time, because it's a slack work time before tobacco housing, and farmers can take off earlier during the day and go to the revival most every night for a week. Our regular preacher helps out, but a different preacher comes in to preach the revival. Sometimes, these new preachers really get excited when they feel the spirit, and sometimes it takes an hour or so for the spirit to really come in.

We usually start the night with the hymn, "Jesus Saves," and we sing it two or three times to get in the religious mood. The words get you to thinking. They go like this: "We have heard the joyful sound; Jesus saves! Jesus saves! Spread the tidings all around; Jesus saves! Jesus saves!" I've always had a good memory, and know many hymns without looking in the book. After the scripture reading, there are long prayers asking Jesus to come into our lives and save us. Some preachers think you should always carry your Bible to follow along with him during the reading. Most women bring their Bible, but most men don't, so they sit there and listen. Then there are more hymns like "Jesus is Calling." When they get to the part that says, "Calling today, Calling today, Jesus is calling, is tenderly calling today," it almost gets you to thinking that he is actually calling you. But the way you get saved is to walk up front during the invitation hymn at the end, and then later you have to get baptized over at the South Licking River.

After the preacher is finished preaching, we sing "Just As I Am." Some preachers keep singing it over and over, if nobody goes up front. When it gets to the part at the end, where they sing real soft like, "I come, I come," it makes you want to step out and go up there. There is so much going through your mind when they sing, "I come, I come," and keep singing it real softly, "I come, I come." But I usually feel scared to go, because people then go up afterwards and shake your hand or hug you, and some of the women cry that you're saved. I think I accept Jesus, but I don't want to be put on the spot up front when the women might come up and cry and hug me.

If nobody goes up front, the preacher stops singing "I come," and tells us to bow our heads and close our eyes, and says, "I want every head bowed and every eye closed." He then starts praying and pleading with Jesus to come into the lost lives. He prays hard and loud at first, but gets soft and gentle toward the end. He then asks for anyone to raise their hand if they want to be prayed for. You're standing there with your eyes closed for a long time, and sometimes I have barely opened my eyes to see if anyone has raised their hands to be prayed for.

I do think about God and Jesus, especially when I'm mowing all day or out somewhere alone. But I don't know how the two of them go together, although they say it's like a father and a son. I used to picture that God was something like my granddad, being older and knowing so much. Maybe Jesus is more like a good uncle, but I don't really know. The pictures of Jesus on our cards at Sunday School usually show him with a clean white robe on and nice long hair all brushed out smooth and sitting around talking to little children. There are not too many pictures of God, and what there are show him as big and mighty. It bothers me, because when I get saved, then am I supposed to let Jesus tell me everything to do and never get to do anything I want to do? What if he told me to not go to picture shows? When it starts bothering me too much, I try to think about playing ball or getting to go to town, but sometimes I think I'll just have to go up front and get it over with.

I'm glad when the revival is over, because things settle down, and I don't have to get cleaned up every night or think as much about if

God still likes me. I can get back to finishing up the summer with tobacco housing time coming and then starting school again and seeing my friends every day. The late August days are still hot ones, but the mornings stay cooler a little longer. The haze and dust kind of linger in the sky longer, and the dew doesn't burn off as quick. The days seem settled and quieter, and the crops are about through growing. It's all like a little signal that tells you it's about time to get crops in the barn and start thinking about getting ready for winter. Before we know it, the dew will turn to frost and the creeks will skim over with ice, and then the snow will be whipping through the cracks in the barn.

Everybody gets to take a little time off in late August to go to the Falmouth Fair, and we never have a revival during fair time. This is a real exciting time, and they have all kinds of lights and shows and rides and games to play to win prizes and races and horse shows. They have hot dogs and soft drinks and popcorn and something new to eat every year. Last year, one booth sold long cut up fried potatoes, and you put catsup on them and ate them just like that. But there is nothing better than getting an ice ball and just walking around and looking at all the rides and everything and hearing the music coming from the merry-go-round. I don't ride the merry-go-round much anymore, but me and my friends like to get on the big Ferris wheel at night and go way up in the dark and then have it stop and look down on all the lights. The air is cool way up there in the night. I like to ride the swings during the day where they swing you around and around on a long chain with a seat, and the wind cools me off. Then when I get off a little dizzy and go get another ice ball, it's so much fun. You can get grape or cherry or lemon or orange syrup on the ice. I like grape the best, but cherry is the prettiest.

My granddad puts on a Sunday shirt and Sunday pants and his good slippers and his Sunday straw hat when he goes to the fair. He likes to just sit under the grandstand roof and watch the cattle and horse shows and talk to the other farmers all sitting there rested. I don't know why he just wants to do that, when he sees cattle and horses every day. They have mule races and different shows and a band that plays. They also have a big barn where there is tobacco and corn and all kinds of things from the garden and sewing and quilts that people show for ribbons and prizes. I never went over there after

I got old enough to go around on my own. There is so much going on at the fair that you don't know what to do. My granddad says that when he was a boy, the fair was the only thing he ever got to do all year. He told me they loaded up real early in the morning in their buggies and spent all day at the fair, and almost everyone in the county was there.

Last year before we left for the fair, my granddad went to the garden and began picking burlap sacks full of sweet corn and putting them in the trunk of the car. I didn't know what he was going to do with all that corn on fair day, but when we got to my uncle's and aunt's house in town, he told me to take a sack down the street and ask the people if they wanted to buy any corn. Well, I did, and before I knew it, every woman was buying corn from me. I sold it all in about an hour and had nearly ten dollars in my pocket. I couldn't believe it. I had the most money I ever had in my life. My mom usually gave me maybe a dollar for the fair each year, and I had to be careful and decide which games and rides and food I would buy. Last year, I was rich, and it was the best fair I ever went to.

My granddad is like that. Sometimes I think all he wants me to do is work. I never know what he might come up with. It's like when he took me out to pick all that corn that morning, when I wanted him to hurry up so we could get to the fair. He didn't tell me why then, but he had it in mind what he was going to do, and now that I think about it, he was thinking about me. I tell you, to walk around that fair with all that money was really something.

At the fair, I usually see some of my school friends that I never see all summer long. It's a time to get together and wander around and see things and know that we'll be back together again soon. Some of my school friends and I get together and just walk around and look at everything. Each year it seems like they have more new things at the fair to see. Last year, off to the side, they had a girl show. We went over there and kind of stood off to the side. There were other men and high school boys standing outside the tent, and two girls came out. They weren't girls, but looked more like they were older, and had on heavy lipstick and jewelry and little tight pants under split-up skirts you could see through. All they had on top was a tight thing that looked like a brassiere, and you could almost see a complete breast. Then a man came out and started some music, and the two girls started dancing around and flinging up their skirts and shaking and smiling at us. The man kept trying to get people to come in, and the girls kept shaking around even more. One of the high school boys said that when you went in, they took off the brassiere and their pants and everything and had on only a real tiny pair of pants underneath so you could even see some of their hair. He said that the man then wanted you to pay extra to see them take off the tiny pair of pants, and that then they would show you how to do it. I never wanted to see a naked woman before, and still don't, because I know my mother would be mad at me, but my friends said we might go in there when we get to high school.

After a couple of days at the fair, it's hard to sit in church the next morning and get my mind back on what God wants me to do. It's hard to get back to work. It's kind of like the fair gets me stirred up, with all the different people and the lights and sounds and the cold drinks and food. On Monday morning early, I'm back in a hot field, and soon I'm thinking about an ice ball and the fun with all my friends. I remember going way down the ridge after the cows in a far pasture one night after being at the fair all day. At the time, I felt so lonely out there with just the cows. I felt like they couldn't understand anything about me, and I wanted to be back with different people and not have to think about so many things. When you're with people, you don't have time to think much, because everybody is talking and laughing. It takes a little time to get myself back into regular life after the fair.

After the tobacco has been topped, the plants get no taller but begin to spread out. Late August is usually a dry time, and without much rain, the tobacco begins to yellow up. If there has been some rain, it stays greener and spreads and thickens. That's what you want a good big, long leaf that will cure up to a golden brown and bring a good price. Shortly after the plants have been topped, little sucker buds begin to grow out where each leaf grows to the stalk. And after two or three weeks, these suckers grow to eight or ten inches. You can't cut the tobacco with these suckers on the stalk, because it won't cure up right and the companies won't buy tobacco with any green suckers in it.

So, you have to break every sucker off the plant. This is one of the real bad jobs with tobacco. You have to walk along and break off each sucker. They are tough and hard to break, and the juice soon cakes your hands with black gum. Even a farmer with the toughest hands will get sores and cracks, and it burns, but the cracks soon get filled with the black gum, so it may not bleed on you. It is a long job, because each plant has anywhere from five to ten suckers that you have to tear off. But it's like everything on the farm. You finish one thing with tobacco, and it's not long until there is something else to do with it. After the suckers are off, you can begin to see the tobacco ripen and turn from green to yellow. The top leaves begin turning first, and then a stalk will slowly ripen down. It's like you took yellow paint out and painted a few leaves every day for a week or two. A field of thick yellow tobacco is sure a pretty sight.

Some farmers get too anxious and go in and began cutting their tobacco when it is still too green. Then it will not cure up right and not bring a good price. A farmer has to know when to do everything at the right time, and not rush it or wait too late. But if it's a late crop year, then you have to worry about frost. A frost makes the leaves splotchy and black, and it can ruin everything. Of course, a summer drought can leave you with spindly plants burnt to a crumbly brown.

When my mother mentions getting school clothes for me and my sister, I know I'll soon be sitting at a desk and not in the field. This takes some getting used to, but I'm anxious to get back in school, because I like school, or most of it. I get some new overalls and some shirts and school shoes. During the war, we got a lot of our things from the Sears, Roebuck catalogue, because we didn't have a car during most of that time. But now, I get to go to town and get some new clothes and feel real good. I get a haircut at the barbershop so as to be all ready for school. Sometimes one of my uncles will cut my hair, to save money or because I can't get to a barbershop.

The tenant kids never go to a barbershop. Their dads don't always do a good job cutting their hair. You can almost always tell tenant kids at school by the way of their haircut, and by the way of their clothes. They almost never have new clothes, and their shoes are bad, but my granddad helps them out, and we give them some of our old clothes and shoes. They never take much to school in their lunch bucket, maybe two biscuits with a piece of cured bacon. Some kids make fun of their haircuts and their clothes. My mother and granddad always say not to make fun of any of them, and it worries me some to see them eat their lunch when it isn't much. We take peanut butter and crackers and maybe marshmallow crème between graham crackers and a cheese sandwich and an apple or pear. Some of the tenant kids don't want to go to school, and they don't. My granddad tells their dads they should send them to school. At school, whenever they have to read out loud in front of the class, it is sometimes bad, and other kids laugh. The teachers don't let them put much arithmetic on the blackboard. Most of them just seem happier to be at the barn or in the field than at school.

Although I work and used to play with these kids every day, I know they're different from us. I know that we're different from a lot of people in the cities and in other parts of the country and the world. I've seen a few foreign people, but not many. We once had a guest preacher from Scotland, and he talked funny. Of course, I've seen pictures of the Japs and seen some of them in the news part at the picture shows. They are really different from us, with their eyes, and they were scary and mean looking during the war. I don't think I've ever seen a real person from China or Japan.

I am around a few Negroes when we go to town. They live in what some people call "Nigger Town," which is over in a corner of Falmouth. My mom says we should never call them "niggers," but call them Negroes or colored people. When I was little, they scared me. One time when I was about six, someone knocked on our door during a hot summer day. It was a Negro man, who was dressed in a suit. I kind of hid back around the living room wall. He said that he had been preaching God's word and was walking to the next town to preach. He asked my mom if she could spare anything to eat, because he was mighty hungry. She said yes, and to come in. She put him at the table on the back porch and went to fix a plate of food for him. She took it to him, and my sister and I waited in the kitchen, because we were a little scared. When she took it to him, we heard him thank her and he then began praying and thanking God for the food and thanking us. We stood there real quiet. He ate everything on the plate, and she also had set a plate of biscuits, some butter, a new pint jar of blackberry jam and a pitcher of milk on the table. He ate all of the biscuits and cleaned out the whole jar of jam and the pitcher of milk. He got up and thanked us again and again and then took off up the road. She told me that he was a nice man.

During the war, all the younger men were off fighting, so it was hard to get farm work done. My granddad hired anyone he could find. He heard that some of the older Negro boys in town would do work. They said most Negroes couldn't pass any of the tests to go in the army. So he got two of them to come to our place and stay for a couple of weeks one summer to help with all the hay and the crops. He talked about where they would sleep, and talked about putting them up the hayloft at the barn, but that was not a good place for people. He put a couple of cots up in the hot attic, which was not a real good place for people either, and they slept there. Some of the neighbors said they would never sit down at a table with niggers, but we let them eat with us. They never said too much, but worked hard and helped us get over the busiest time.

I don't know if other people feel uneasy around strangers or people not like us, but I do. I even feel a little uneasy around city people. And I feel uneasy around people with a college education, except my teachers. Some of the teachers don't have much college education and some don't act like it, so they seem like us most of the time. As I get older, I know I will have to quit feeling uneasy if I ever expect to go off to college and get an easy office job.

Sometimes, though, I think I may not want an office job like a lawyer. On a hot day out loading hay on a wagon all day with the dust and the dry leaves falling down and sticking to my back, I think of a way to do something easier. Many times, I've told Crit and Sollie that someday I'll be sitting in an office with an electric fan blowing air on me and making good easy money. But out there in the field with the birds and all the many things that nature brings, it's an easy and free feeling, and I don't have to be clean all the time or be careful how I talk. I don't know what I will ever do, but my granddad says I need to keep learning how to do everything, but most of all not be afraid of work.

## CHAPTER EIGHT

## CUTTING AND HOUSING TIME

Our school starts each year at around tobacco housing time. School work is a lot different from farm work, and book learning is a lot different from learning how to shear a sheep. School takes some getting used to and settling down. I'll be in the eighth grade and big enough with the other boys in the eighth grade to be kind of the king of our school. There will be about eight or ten in my class if they all come back. My sister will be in the seventh grade and will be in the same room with me this year. Some of the older boys will not start school until all the tobacco is in, and it can be two or three weeks later. During tobacco housing time, the teachers don't give you too much work to do or go too fast with the lessons, because they know the boys and some of the girls will be working late each night at the barn housing tobacco and then having to milk late. But it's sure different to change from all the work to just sitting all day. Some of the seventh and eighth-grade boys get squirmy if they sit too long and have to pay attention. But last year, we made a basketball court outside, and it is wonderful. We can't wait for recess and noon so we can go out there and play.

We kept asking Miss Carrie if we could put up two goals outside to make a court, and she said we could if we could get somebody to do it, because schools never have money to get anything except a few books. Miss Carrie teaches the seventh and eighth grades together, and she is head of the school. So one day Lloyd Turner, an older eighth grader, went home after school, took his dad's truck and brought two long locust posts to school and dumped them out on the ground. The next day we began putting them up and then made backboards for the goals. We were so happy that Lloyd brought those poles for the goals, and we made our court and even put white lime down for the out of bounds. I really like to shoot basketball, and we choose up and play games. It is the best thing I ever like to do. Miss Carrie said that we might get to play against another school in the county, and that will sure make school a lot better.

When the tobacco gets ripe and turns to a golden-yellow color, it's time for cutting and housing. Housing means to put it in the barn. I don't know why we call it housing when we haul it and hang it in a barn, but we do. It's the most important time of the year, and it's one of the hardest times of the year. Cutting tobacco is really hard to do, and not everybody can do it. In a way, it's like shooting a basketball. Some people are good and can make a lot of goals, and some seldom ever make any. It's kind of hard to explain, but some men can shoot the eyes out of a squirrel in a tall treetop with a 22 rifle and some can never hit one. So in tobacco cutting, you have to hit the spear with a cut stalk, and if you're not any good at this, it will take forever.

You almost have to see it to understand how to cut tobacco, but I'll try to explain it the best way I can with words. First of all, you have to drop tobacco sticks in each row. A tobacco stick is about four feet long and about the size of a big man's thumb. The ends of each stick are sharpened so that one end can be stuck in the ground and so that a spear will fit over the other end. A spear is like the shape of a small cone for ice cream. It is made out of hard steel and the point is always kept as sharp as a needle.

What you have to do is stick the stick in the ground and put the spear over the end sticking up. Then you cut the tobacco stalk off down near the ground with a very sharp tobacco knife that we call a tomahawk. You then slam the stalk over the spear so that it slides down the stick and stays there. You have to hit the spear just right so the stalk doesn't split out and fall off the stick. A good tobacco cutter can hit the spear just right nearly every time. A bad cutter has to keep trying to hit the spear, and it takes forever to get to the end of a row. It's like hitting eight out of ten free throws in basketball, or making only one or two. Some people can do it, and some just keep fooling around. After spearing six stalks on a stick, you pick up another stick, stick it in the ground, put the spear over the end and go on and spear six other stalks. You have to be very careful, because the spear is dangerous and the tomahawk is dangerous, and when you're moving fast and not paying attention, you can cut your foot or leg with the tomahawk or spear your arm. One time, when one of my cousins was cutting, the stick fell over just as he was ready to spear a stalk and the spear went through his ear. I've seen men spear their arms and hands when they got too fast and careless.

The important part is to learn how to cut fast. The best way is to stick the stick in the ground so that it is slanted and the spear end is about three feet from the ground. That way you never have to keep raising up and down. You can cut the stalk and with one quick, smooth motion, spear it and then cut another and keep going on and on without ever raising up. A cutter who sticks the stick straight up has to raise up and down when cutting and spearing every stalk and this takes forever.

I started cutting a little last year, and I'm getting pretty good at it, but my mother is still afraid I'll spear myself, especially because it's is so hard to do. It seems we always get a real hot spell during cutting time, and when you're bent over all day down under the tobacco plants and there is no air, it gets to you and you get mighty tired. At church or at the store, the men talk about who the good tobacco cutters are. A good cutter can cut and spear up to 1,000 sticks a day. I think I'll be a good one some day, but staying bent over all day makes you glad that school is about ready to start. Crit and Sollie and our other farm hands always have to go easy at first until they can get toughened up. My granddad can't cut anymore, because of his joints, so he helps drop sticks through the rows or goes to get the barn ready for housing or maybe checks on the sheep.

Cutting is about the hardest thing you have to do on a farm as I said, but housing is not that easy either. After the tobacco is cut and has wilted a day or two in the hot sun, it is ready for the barn. If it has been a good crop year, then the tobacco is big and heavy. Six big stalks on a stick make it pretty heavy, but that's what you want. You have to hand each full stick up on the wagon, and the loader takes each stick and very gentle like so as to not break or bruise the leaves, stacks it neatly on the wagon. Of course, it's harder on the kids to lift a heavy full stick up to the wagon, but we have to do it, because everybody has to pitch in at tobacco housing time. Load after load is then taken to the tobacco barn to hang and dry. It's like you're taking valuable things, so you handle it easy and very carefully, knowing it's most of your money for the year.

The tobacco barns are built different from any other barn. It's like if you built a barn completely empty with no stalls or no hayloft or anything inside. Then when it had the roof on and all the sides up, you went in and took tier-poles about 15 feet long and nailed them all up through the barn so that the tobacco sticks could be hung all in a row to dry. The tier-poles are put about four feet wide and four feet high so that you have rows all the way through the barn. Most tobacco barns are four or five tiers high. You can hang four or five rows of tobacco down through a barn with each row over the top of another one. You bring a wagon full into the barn and send two or three men up into the tiers and begin handing up each stick of tobacco. The men have to spread out wide with a foot placed on each tier or rail as we call them. Each rail is four feet apart. You then hand up each stick to the first man, and he hands it up to the man right above him and on and on and up and up. The men then have to place each stick about eight inches apart and spread and shake each plant that has been speared on the stick. It has to be spread so it will get air and cure up right and not rot.

You keep moving through the barn rails, hanging and shaking and spreading the stalks. It's hard to keep raising it all up above your head hour after hour. And it is dangerous, because you're spread out wide with your feet and bending over and raising up and down and moving backward down the wobbly rails. You have to be real careful not to lose your balance and fall out, which could be 20 to 30 feet to the ground. Hanging tobacco is one thing a boy can't do until his legs are long enough to spread out far enough to reach from one rail to another.

Whenever I had anyone to play with when I was little, we always liked to go to the tobacco barn and climb around way up in the rails. We would play monkeys or Tarzan and climb all over. My mother would be scared if she knew we were in the tobacco barn, and never wanted my granddad to let me go there by myself and climb. When I was little, there were lots of ways to play at the barns. Whenever we had boys or relatives from town come, they wouldn't know what to do at the barns. There was so much to do that I wondered what they ever did in towns where they didn't have barns. We played hide and seek in the haylofts and covered ourselves with hay. We had corncob fights and climbed around and shot at sparrows with our slingshots.

One time a neighbor brought his city grandkid over who was visiting, and I took him out and showed him how we had corncob fights. Well, I was pretty good and knew how to throw hard, and he had little cuts and welts all over his face when we were through. His mother was pretty mad when she saw him. It was fun to take town kids out with nice clothes and shoes on and then go wade in the blue-mud pond and run and throw stuff and climb. When we went to the house, their mothers would be shocked at how they looked. It never bothered me too much to get cow manure on me. But when they did, after romping and rassling around in the barn, their mothers would go wash them off right then.

A big barn full of curing tobacco hanging there all neat and straight is a pretty sight and a big relief. The hardest part is over for the year. But you're never through worrying about it or taking care of everything you have, especially the tobacco crop. My granddad checks the tobacco out every day, and opens or closes the barn doors depending on the weather and how much air the tobacco needs to cure up as pretty as it can. The weather is always important to everything growing and curing. In very late crop years, cutting and housing can come so late that frost, which ruins tobacco in the field, is a big worry. A late crop may not cure up soon enough before an early freeze, which would also ruin a crop in the barn. I remember one time, when we were expecting an early freeze, my granddad had us go bring all our sheep in the tobacco barn for the night. He said that the heat from the sheep would keep the barn warm enough to not freeze the tobacco.

It seems like everything is good some of the time and then bad some of the time. It's always very good to finally have a tobacco crop hanging in the barn. Then something happens to make things turn out bad. The sheep can be doing well and nothing bothering them, and then out of nowhere, the dogs get in them and kill and mangle some. A good cow can suddenly get down and then die for no good reason, and you've lost something valuable. A fox can get in the hen house and a horse can come up lame. The mowing machine can break or Crit can get a bad pain in his side.

I think the bad things bother my granddad, more than he lets on, but he never gets so disgusted that he says too much about it. He does have a lot on his mind with taking care of everything every day and trying to figure out how to do the best at farming. He has to tell our tenants what to do every day, and decide when is the best time to cut hay or top tobacco or do anything. I've noticed that Crit and Sollie don't have many of these worries. They are happy nearly every day, and never seem to have too much on their mind.

When we're out doing something like chopping out tobacco and get to the end of a row, it's fun to sit under a shade tree and rest for a few minutes and get water. They might roll a cigarette or put in a fresh chew and just sit there and talk about the woodpecker over in a nearby tree or one of their dogs howling and on the trail of a rabbit over in a hollow. While we're sitting there in the shade, Crit might say, "I think that old dog is close to a rabbit, listen to him." And Sollie might then say, "Sounds like he's on a squirrel to me or a groundhog, he's not barking like it's a rabbit." They see and hear a lot more things than I do. They'll even play with a doodle bug while we're sitting there or watch all the goings on at an ant hill. Whenever we stop for a while, Sollie usually takes out his sharp pocketknife and starts whittling on a piece of wood, and he will keep whittling out a little something as long as we sit there. I think he could be happy the rest of his life under a tree or sitting on a milk stool at the barn whittling and spitting his tobacco juice out every now and then. I guess he knows how to keep his mind at ease.

When school starts in mid-September, the days get clearer and the air has cooled down. The early morning haze keeps the sun hidden longer, but when it breaks through, the sky is as blue as it can get. The leaves on the trees are quieter as the summer winds blow away. The leaves begin fading and losing the deep green color. The grass and pasture fields have nearly stopped growing, and the hills seem smoother as the grass and wildflowers begin bending over to lie down in getting ready for winter's sleep. On some of the early cool mornings, I need a light jacket when I go get Lady for my granddad.

The early fall is a clear time and a different time. I have to change back from hard work every day to doing lessons. After early morning work, I go in and wash my face and hands and put on a little hair tonic with some water and then go to the road for the school bus, or sometimes ride to school with our milk truck driver, Pete. It sure feels different with my good clothes on, and it sure is different to go from housing tobacco to spelling words and reading from books. At recess and noon, we go out to our new basketball court, choose up and play a game. If it's a warm day, we get all sweaty and dusty, and then the bell rings and we go back to our seats. The teacher tries to settle us down to get back to the book work, and our papers get smeared with sweat, and most of the boys are thinking about after school when they can get back to where it's free and they feel easy.

After school, my granddad always has something for me to do before milking time. Sometimes I get a little time in between, so I always go shoot ball at my goal fastened to the barn. I'd rather shoot ball than anything I know. That way, I can go way off and think I'm in a big game in a gym, hearing all the people cheer when I make a goal. When we get to play another school in the county this year, I'll be happy, and I can't wait to get to high school next year, so I have to keep shooting all I can.

In the early fall, most of the garden is gone. We have a few green beans and a few other things I have to pick, but in the fall, we go back to soup beans mostly, and then later in the winter, my mother cooks the green beans she canned in the summer. If it has been a good year for fruit, I have to pick the apples and pears, and my mother makes apple and pear butter. I always have to gather walnuts and hickory nuts, and my mother uses them for cookies, cakes and some candy through the winter. We gather any type food we can, because of money.

A few years ago, when I was about in the fourth or fifth grade, my granddad told me to get all the walnuts from the grove down past the chicken house and to bring them up and hull them for winter. I went down, picked them up and carried several sacks full up to the barn lot. Now, a walnut has a hull on the outside and it's thick and green but not real hard. Inside the hull is the hard shell of the walnut, which keeps the meat good all winter. You have to take the soft hull off so the walnut will dry out and keep. At school, boys never like to go to school with walnut stain on them, because other kids laugh. When you hull walnuts, you have to break the green hull with a hammer or rock and then tear off the hull with your hands so the hard shell underneath will keep. Well, whenever you start tearing off the hull, the juice gets all over your hands. It stains your hands with a dark green and brown stain, and you cannot wash it off. The stain takes two or three weeks to wear off, so your hands are stained real dark. There were a few kids that would say you had nigger hands, but the teachers better not hear you say this.

I was real worried and did not want to get my hands all stained, and did not know what to do. It worried me so much that I began throwing a lot of the walnuts over the hill so I wouldn't get too much stain on me. One day my granddad asked if I had hulled all the walnuts, and I said yes. Then he took me by the arm and led me down by the chicken house and picked up a few of the walnuts that I had thrown down there, and said, "No, you didn't, and why did you lie to me?" I was never so scared in my life, and I never saw him act that way. He took me up by the chicken house and cut a switch off a willow tree, and I was so scared that my mind couldn't think at all. I knew I shouldn't have thrown the walnuts away, but I didn't know what to do if the other kids made fun of me.

My granddad had never whipped me before. He may have hit me a little with a belt real easy a time or two or with his razor strop when I was real little. But he had never given me a real whipping. I always knew that I could not ever lie, though. I don't know how I learned this, but I always knew it. My mom and my granddad and my uncles always taught us the right things from the start.

I didn't want the other kids to laugh at me, and didn't know what to do about it except throw some of the walnuts down over the hill and not make my hands look so bad. I was so scared when he cut the switch that I was crying and shaking and felt so bad. I felt worse than I ever felt before. I never wanted him mad at me ever, and I was so scared it would hurt me real bad, and I thought about my mom and the kids at school and lots of things all at once.

He maybe hit me three or four times across the back of my legs with the switch. I can't remember. He didn't hit me too hard, and it was over with quick. Then he said, "Now don't ever lie to me again." I never will again, I know that for sure. He never told my mother that I know of, and I never told anybody until now. It hurt me in so many ways, but I don't remember too much about it now only the real scary part. I try not to think about it, but I know one thing about lying. It will always cause trouble.

From that day on, I never have to think about trying to get out of doing something that I don't want to do. But I've noticed that I'm thinking more about when I don't want to go along with my granddad. It's not that I don't respect him or like him, but I want to do different things besides work. Some of the boys drive cars and trucks, and want to be around girls more, and the high school boys go out on Saturday nights and drive fast and take girls for rides and sometimes park out on a side road and try to mess with them. Some of the boys are pretty wild and smoke and go get beer and wreck their cars. I hear them talk about this all the time. When we have to go to church on Sunday nights, the boys like to get in somebody's car and sit and play the radio and talk before we go in. The older boys tell me all about the things they do, and I know my mom and granddad would never let me slip off and do some of these things. And I don't want to do them, but I wonder if I might when I get old enough.

I don't like to go to Sunday school and church as much as I did, but we go every Sunday morning and Sunday night. In the winter, we go to prayer meeting on Wednesday nights. We don't have prayer meeting in the summer, because farmers are working almost right up to dark. Sometimes we have prayer meetings in people's houses when it's cold, because they don't have to go and build a fire at the church. At prayer meetings, we start off with prayers and then study the Bible. The kids have to sit there and listen too, but I used to like it when the preacher was telling about some king or Moses or the Red Sea. At school, I like to learn about history and geography. One time, at prayer meeting, the preacher was explaining something about Egypt. He asked if anyone knew what they called it when a river spread out into several rivers like the Nile River does before it empties into the sea. Nobody said anything, and I knew the answer, but was afraid to say anything. And then I said, "It's a delta," and he said, "right." All the people kind of stopped and looked at me. I was a little scared, but knew the people thought I was maybe pretty smart to know that, and I was proud to finally up and say something in front of all the older people.

At the prayer meetings in the winter, sometimes we have oyster soup or some other soup and crackers, and each woman bakes a pie to take. After studying the Bible, we eat and talk and have fun. But I don't like church as much as I used to. I know I shouldn't be more interested in sitting in a car and talking to the boys, but I also don't want to be around older people so much any more. Church is all right, but you can only learn so many lessons, and you get tired of it with the same thing over and over. The preachers get excited and keep trying to save everybody's soul and get people to stop sinning so much. They get some kind of spirit in them as they go along and build up and holler and sweat if it's a warm day. It seems like they get real loud whenever they get started on the Devil. I never think too much about the Devil, because I just can't figure it all out with God in heaven and the Devil in hell and both of them against each other. I wonder why God didn't destroy the Devil if he was so powerful that he could do everything else. But when I don't go to church for some reason, and the preacher says it makes the Devil happy, then I feel that maybe God will make my life harder or punish me.

My granddad says that after Sundays everybody goes right back to doing what they've been doing and they forget all about church until the next week. He never talks any about Jesus or very much about church, so I don't know what he really thinks. What he does every Sunday morning after milking is go put on his Sunday clothes and, if it's summer, take his Sunday school lesson book out under the pear tree and read it for awhile. You can see him read a little bit and then look away like he's thinking about it. He never tells anybody about what he really thinks or believes about it all. He never says the dinner blessing when we have company, and I've never heard him pray out loud. He just reads a lesson every Sunday and then goes to church and comes home and that's it. He doesn't say anything about what the preacher preached or anything.

It's like when he's out with his sheep. He just likes to look at them and study them, and you know he's thinking about them all quiet like. He's like that when he's reading his Sunday school lesson under the pear tree. He looks at it for a while, and then looks up like he's wondering what it all means. You know he's thinking about it with the way he's so quiet and off to himself. He may be in church in a way when he's out with his sheep. There is no need to say anything. I guess God knows what we're thinking whether we say anything or not.

My granddad grew up under the old ways, and he keeps doing most everything the old way. When he was a boy, he almost never got to go to town. They did when it was time for the fair, and they went to church every Sunday and the store once in a while. But he mostly worked with his brothers when he was young and went to school only a little for about four or five years. He said they only needed to learn how to read and write and do some figuring back then. The important thing was working the farm to make a living and feeding a big family.

They did everything the old way in the Bible. It talks about sowing and reaping and shepherds and flocks and the sweat of your brow. That's how my granddad lives. He seems to feel better doing everything like it always was. Some of the preachers preach against the modern ways of living. I don't think my granddad thinks the new ways are bad or he is set too much in his ways. He does try to do farm things the new way when the county agent tells him about new seeds or new ways to doctor the sheep. He just seems to hesitate to jump in too quick and do anything with the new machinery they have now. He doesn't understand much about the new machinery, and seems to be leery of anything with a motor.

After the war, some of the soldiers came back and started getting tractors and machinery for their farms. They can plow and mow and disk more land in a day than we can in a week with the horses. A few of the younger farmers are starting to bale their hay, and this way is much faster than the old way of pitching every straw with a pitchfork. I've driven a tractor a couple of times, and it is a wonderful feeling with all that power. It's so easy to sit up there and move on across a hay field so fast. I've asked my granddad many times to think about getting a big red Farmall H or a pretty green John Deere, but he seems to maybe be afraid of knowing how to use one. I tell him I could drive it and do so much more work, but he's uneasy about it all. They cost a lot, and we always have to be very careful with our money.

Last fall, I was happy, because he bought an old school bus that the county schools sold after it had almost worn out. It was a big, long International and I was excited. A few of the neighbors have a truck, and we could see how much more hay they could haul and even take their own lambs and cattle to the stock yards to sell. The day we got the big old bus was one of my happiest days in a long time. I thought about how big I would feel driving up over a big steep hill with a full load of hay. When we got it home, a neighbor's tenant, Leonard Hall, who knows something about motors and everything, came over and cut the top and sides off with a chisel. He made it into a regular truck with a flat bed and racks that we can put on to haul stock. I felt so good that my granddad was finally going to let us do some of the new ways.

Up until I was about seven, we didn't have electricity. We got it about the time the war started, and we were lucky. When the war

117

broke out, they stopped stretching out the lines, and the people who lived up the road from us had to wait until last year before they got electricity. I'm sure glad we got it. At first, all we had were the light bulbs. We didn't get much else that worked on electricity, because they didn't make many new things during the war except fighting equipment. We did get an electric radio, which was better than the old battery radio that gave out all the time. I think the best thing about electricity now is the refrigerator and the cold water and drinks and ice, especially in the hot summer time. Well water or spring water is cool and good, but cistern water gets a little warm and stale-like in the summer. There is nothing better than coming in from a hot hayfield at dinnertime and having a big cold pitcher of tea or lemonade on the table and ice cubes in your glass.

Some people still want to do everything the old way. When they were putting in the electric lines back before the war, some of the older farmers wouldn't let the company set the poles or stretch the lines across their land. It was a fight, like many other things. Some were plain contrary, but some were afraid, or said they were. They said the electric lines might fall down and cause a hay field to burn up or burn up their house or barn.

A few of the bigger dairy farmers started getting milking machines after the war. We were surprised that an electric machine could actually milk a cow, and we went to see one. Milking is not that hard, but it takes a lot of time, and you have to do it morning and night every day. A milking machine can milk much quicker than you can by sitting and squeezing on a cow's tits all the time. My granddad has talked a little about getting one, but I don't know if he will.

The electric light bulbs are much better than a kerosene lamp, and it's easier to read at nights. My mother has it easier with the electric stove that we got last year. They didn't make electric stoves during the war. We used to use a big old wood cook stove, and it would get very hot in the kitchen in the summer time. When she was canning beans and everything in the summer, it stayed hot and we always ate on the back porch to stay away from the cook stove. Some of the farms have a summer kitchen outside the house, but we never did and I don't know why. It's a little building out and away from the house. That way, you don't heat up the house as much. We did have a kerosene cook stove for a few years before we got the electric cook stove, and it was easier than a wood stove and didn't heat up the kitchen as much.

Some of the houses are putting in running water, where electricity pumps water from a cistern right into your sink, and all you have to do is turn a faucet. Some even have an electric water heater, so you don't have to heat up a kettle on the stove. We don't have electricity pumping water in our house. You can't get everything. We still have a hand pump at the kitchen sink, which pumps water from the cistern and, it's not that bad. When we want water, we don't have to go out to the cistern and draw water out of it with a rope and bucket like a lot of people still do. A couple of the farm houses around here are starting to put bathrooms right in the house with tubs and showers and a commode. Some of the older farmers say they would never take a shit in their house. Of course, most of the women use the outhouse. Ours is out a little ways behind our smoke house. But most men still take a dump down in a holler or in the bushes somewhere. I guess it all is what you get used to. A shower would feel good after coming in from a hot hayfield. You could get all the sticky leaves and dust off so easy. I've been in a shower a few times, and I like to just stand there and let it run all over me. That's what I'm looking forward to when I get to Morgan High School and can take a shower every day after basketball practice.

The best thing about electricity is the cold refrigerator. We did have the iceman come by once a week and sell us a big chunk for our icebox out on the back porch. We could keep milk and butter fairly cold and some other things. The tenants never have ice in the summer. They have to keep their milk and butter down in a cistern to keep it a little cool and from spoiling, and they never have a cold drink except when going to the store. They put their milk and stuff in a tin bucket with a tight lid and let it down in the cistern with a rope. Whenever I go to the store with them, the first thing we do is to get a cold soft drink. Boy, that is so good. When we're out working in the sun and know we'll go to the store that night, we talk about which soft drink we'll get. The men like big Pepsis the best, and women like Cokes. Sometimes stores get new soft drinks like RC or Dr. Pepper, and then they came out with orange and red crème soda, which they called Jersey Crème, and a little grape drink called Grapette. Kids like orange probably the best, or Jersey Creme. For a long time, I liked

Grapette the best. When refrigerators came out, some people started buying soft drinks for their homes. My granddad says soft drinks cost too much to keep at home and that too many of them are bad for you. So we have mostly tea and cold milk for drinks at dinner and supper and coffee for breakfast. He never likes to eat or drink much of anything that is store bought. He thinks most of it is bad for you.

Our telephones are getting better too. Before the war we had the old hand-crank telephone. Now we have a modern one that you just dial with numbers. It's on what they call a party line, which means that six or eight neighbors can listen in to what we say when we talk on the phone, and we can listen to them if we take up the receiver. It rings different for each house. Our ring is three long rings. If it rings two longs, it's for Raymond Loomis down the road. So when it rings two long rings, you can pick up the receiver and listen to what Raymond or his wife or kids are saying. You can tell when a neighbor is listening in, because you can hear a click, and sometimes you can hear their breathing. Some of the neighbor women listen in all the time, because they are so nosy and want to know everything about gossip in the community. Everybody is disgusted with two of my great uncles who farm down the road. Every morning at about 5:00 they call each other to see what farm work they're going to do that day. So everybody's phone rings in their house at about 5:00 every morning and wakes everybody up whether they want to or not.

It seems like many things changed after the war. They really had to invent a lot of new things and make planes and tanks and guns better than the Germans and the Japs did. We won the war, and now you can see how many of these new things are coming into how we live. They're even talking about how farmers might use Jeeps now to do some of the work. I just wish we could move on with tractors and balers and everything, and quit doing everything the old way. The old way is the hard way, and too slow. My granddad might see that I can drive a tractor and get much more done. But he still doesn't know about it all, or he needs a little more time to study it. I love to drive our truck up over a hill and to the barn with more hay on it than we could put on three wagons. It makes me feel big and powerful. I think he now sees that I am growing up a little.

He knows so much about everything else, but when a motor stops or machinery doesn't work right, he says, "I might as well look up a hoss's ass." It's funny the way he says it. If the truck stops and we put up the hood, he will always look in and say, "I might as well look up a hoss's ass." Crit and Sollie don't know anything about motors either. When you don't know much about all the new things, it's easier to go on like you always have. I know that in my future I can't keep doing everything his old way. If I go on to school and college, I will have to learn a lot more about all the new things.

When you sit on a mowing machine with the horses pulling it along all day, you don't have to think about problems in the world or motors not working or another war. It's just the sun, the birds, the little rabbits and sometimes snakes scurrying about. It gives you time to wonder about everything out over the world. But you can kind of stay where you are, and it seems easier to do than trying something a lot different. Sometimes you'll be mowing along and a meadowlark will start flying and darting around the mowing machine and chirping a crying sound. You know she's trying to tell you that you're getting too close to her nest. But you have to go on. You can't stop and look for the nest and mow around it. If there were more time, you wouldn't have to disturb anything. I often wish I never had to disturb anything.

# CHAPTER NINE

## SOON BE TIME FOR WINTER WOOD

When the tobacco hanging in the barn is drying up real pretty, and the grass in the pasture fields begins losing its deep-green tint and the leaves on the trees begin to fade, it's time to start getting ready for winter. Everything goes out in the spring and comes in during the fall. The seeds, the plants, and the animals all go out to meet with the warming earth in the spring. Then as summer comes along, our barns begin to be lonely places. We still milk in the barn, and bring the horses in for harnessing in the mornings and feed them some ears of corn in their stalls during dinnertime, but our barns are bare most of the time during the summer. Of course, we're putting up hay all through the summer, so we spend some hot times in the steaming lofts. But it seems like we no sooner get everything settled outside for the summer, and then we have to start thinking about getting everything back in for the winter.

A family can live from a good garden in the summer, but in the winter the food comes from a cellar full of canned food and potatoes and the smokehouse with cured meat hanging from the rafters. With eggs from the hen house, frying chickens from the brood house and fresh milk from the milk house, you don't need much else. A cured ham or shoulder from the smokehouse now and then gives a change from all the summer-fried chicken. The big slabs of cured bacon sliced up thick with eggs and biscuits after morning milking is enough to keep you going till dinner.

My mother cans everything she can all summer long, and, of course, my sister helps her with it all. By September, the shelves in our cool cellar under the house are lined with jars and jars of fruit and vegetables. The many different colors all lined up on the shelves down in the cool, damp cellar made it look neat and good. There are dark-red pickled beets, bright-yellow corn kernels, light-green pickle relish, deep-purple blackberries, bright-red cherries, blood-red tomatoes, light-green lima beans, dark-green green beans, and light-green peas. She makes a chili sauce out of tomatoes, peppers and onions, and it sure tastes good when poured over a bowl of stew meat.

122

Whenever I get to eat in town, orange juice tastes about the best of anything I could ever swallow. We seldom have any oranges, so my mother makes jars and jars of tomato juice, and we use it all through a winter. We never have to worry about having enough tomatoes in the summer. On the front shelves in the cellar, she stores little jars of many kinds of jam, jelly and preserves. We may have raspberry, strawberry, blackberry, gooseberry, cherry, plum, peach and pear and apple butter. My granddad also likes his sorghum or honey on biscuits soaked with bright yellow butter at the end of a meal. All farmers and hands have to have their sweetening with a meal. Soup beans with onions, cornbread and a big hunk of meat makes a good winter dinner. But in summer, green beans with new potatoes, corn on the cob, tomatoes, onions and cucumbers with fried chicken and gravy get you ready for an afternoon's work. The sweetening at the end of every meal gives the little extra to get you through till supper.

We eat little new potatoes in the summer, which are big enough about mid-June. The peas come on at about the same time, so my mother fixes up a big pot of little new potatoes mixed with fresh peas. She cooks them in a cream sauce, and they are sure good. Everything seems to come on just right. We have lettuce and onions from the tobacco bed in the early spring, strawberries in late May, the first tomato in mid-July and the big juicy pears and apples in the fall. It all works out just about right. It's like whenever you really start craving a big red juicy tomato, nature begins turning one on a vine.

The bottom bin in the cellar is for the late potatoes. If they dry out right, there might be enough to last for most of the winter. My granddad also keeps tins of mutton tallow in the cellar. When he slaughters a lamb or mutton for meat, he renders some of the fat for the tallow. He uses it for many things: to soften leather harness, and to soften and cure a cow's split or raw tit. In the winter, sometimes a cow's tit splits and bleeds and gets very sore. It's no fun trying to milk a cow when she doesn't want you to grab and start jerking on her sore tit. The mutton tallow is good for softening and healing. We put it on the horses' shoulders where their collar for the harness has rubbed and caused a sore. My granddad uses it for his hands when they get dried out and split. It's good for a lot of things, but it sure smells awful, and I never liked it rubbed on me.

People know what works for certain ailments. We seldom ever have any real medicine from a doctor. My mother keeps a bottle of Vick's salve in the winter. When my sister or I get a cold or the croup, she rubs it on our chest and puts hot towels over it to soak it in. She thinks it will loosen up our breathing. It smells bad too, and now that I'm older, I don't want to go to school smelling like Vick's salve. In the very early spring, my granddad goes out and digs up some sassafras roots, and my mother boils them to make sassafras tea. The tea is a real deep reddish-brown and smells and tastes good on a cold day. It's supposed to thin your blood and make you feel livelier after a hard winter. I don't know if it does or not. If somebody gets cut pretty deep with an ax or hatchet, we soak the cut in coal oil and wrap it in a clean cloth. Coal oil takes the sting out and cures it up pretty good. We never actually go to a doctor unless something is real bad.

My granddad doctors his sheep whenever they need it. He can always tell when one is looking puny. When we started doping them with phenothiazine three or four times a year, it cleared up their stomach worms real well. He never wants to see a ewe or lamb sickly like.

In early August, we take a day and bring all the ewes and bucks to the barn to get ready for breeding. Of course, we keep the ewes and bucks in separate fields year round except when we get ready to breed them. We sort them and dope them again, and my granddad figures out which ewes to be put with which buck to breed. We also put a dab of paint on each one of them at the time so we can tell which sheep is ours if they get over into a neighbor's field. We use a dab of green paint up between the shoulders. A neighbor might use a dab of red paint on a rear hip or somewhere else.

Turning the bucks in with the ewes is a day to work in a cool barn out of the sun, but when we turn them out into a field, things get hot. The bucks go right to work, and it seems like they don't know which ewe to mount and stick, because they run from one to the other and smell one and then another one. They'll even start smelling a ewe's rear end in the barn lot before we can get them to a field. It's kind of fun in a way to watch them get all flustered. Crit might say, "If it's cool tonight, that old buck might have to work real hard." The first day or two after turning in the bucks, they wear out and just lie around in the shade because of so much breeding.

We wean the lambs in early June so it will give the ewes a couple of months to get in good shape for breeding and starting all over again to carry a lamb or two inside them and then give birth and give milk for the next several months. It wears out a ewe to keep giving milk too long. By August, they're in good shape and ready for the buck.

I've known how animals breed for a long time, and nobody ever told me, because I watched it. I know how people breed too, but don't think about it too much and don't talk about it. I do hear the older boys talk about it, and some of the older high school boys say they are getting a little, but it makes me feel a little shy about it all. Some of the older boys even carry rubbers in their billfolds, and I don't know if I ever will or not. Sometimes if my sister has a girlfriend come to stay all night and we are playing around and romping and I touch her or something, it does make me wonder, and I might think a little about breeding. But I don't think too much about it yet.

It does get interesting to watch animals breed, but after a while, it doesn't amount to that much. Horses get the most excited when they breed. We've bred a few mares and once bred Lady to a good saddle stud and got a pretty little colt from her. I think little colts are the cutest of all baby things. Whenever you take a mare in heat to a big stud horse, the stud goes crazy. He will almost tear up a stall until he can get on top of the mare. And he goes at it fast and can't wait till it's over. Bulls get a little excited, but don't act as wild as a stud horse. You have to be careful that a big bull doesn't get with a little heifer and breed her. A big bull can break down a little heifer with all his weight, so there is always something to watch about animals. Some bulls will break down a fence to get to a pretty young heifer, and you have to make sure he's in a field with a strong fence. I don't know how many times a rooster does it, but it seems like they're on top of a hen several times a day. The funniest breeding is the ducks. They'll be swimming around the pond, and then the male will get on top and practically drown the female until he's through. When he's through, he'll get off and swim around the female in a circle three or four times real quick. It's like he's bragging. I never like to watch dogs breed, because it seems there is something disgusting about it, and cats never like to do it when people are around. They breed mostly at night. Everything else is interesting to watch, because it makes you think about how nature works. Breeding is the one time when a stud horse or a bull or a buck gets excited and acts a little crazy. The older boys act a little crazy too when they talk about getting some.

A good buck sheep can breed about 25 ewes. We have five bucks for our 120 ewes. It takes a buck about a month to breed all 25, so it's about one a day or something like that, and the lambs start coming about five months later in January. At first, they come steady, and then it slows down. I guess that's because the bucks wear down after so much breeding when it's so hot in August. Crit and Sollie laugh about the worn-out bucks, and sometimes will say something like, "I'm about as tired as that old buck sheep there lying in the shade and panting." The lambs usually come all through the month of January so it makes it easier to take care of them all if there are any problems. Then the lambs are ready for market in late spring and early summer when people in the cities want a good leg of lamb to roast for their holidays. When you think about it, nature kind of takes care of things by even getting the bucks too tired to breed every ewe too fast. Lambing time is spread out so we can handle it.

After about a month when every ewe should be bred, we separate the bucks and ewes again. Most of our ewes are what are called Western cross. They are a crossbreed with some Hampshire blood in them and are big-boned and rangy. We used to use Hampshire bucks, which are big bony sheep with long black faces. We have also used Dorset bucks, which have a white face and big curly horns, but now we use Southdown bucks. They are short and squatty and even smaller than some of the ewes. But they produce a very good lamb that sells real well. The meat is good and tender, and people must like a roast from a Southdown. After breeding time, we're through with the sheep until bad weather comes in December and the pickings get slim in the pastures. Then we give them a little hay and a little grain to fatten them up for giving birth. My granddad rides out most every day to check on them. He takes out a little salt or grain now and then to keep them familiar with him so when he calls, they come.

Toward the end of September, I get pretty used to school and settled down some. The cooler days make it easier to get my mind on the lessons, and the work on the farm slows down. Of course, I still have things to do every day after school, but it's not as rushed as in the summer, and I have a little time to shoot basketball some days before or after milking before it gets dark. We have more school work in the winter when we're in the house more, because the teachers know they won't get much done until the tobacco is all housed. But with two grades in each room, we could do most all our work while the teacher is having a lesson with the other grade. If we have ten spelling words for the next day, I can look at them a time or two while she is explaining something to the other grade and I can memorize them quick and not have to take them home. We have two or three shelves of reading books that we can take home and read on our own, which don't have anything to do with the lesson books. I am kind of interested in the history ones. At Morgan High School, they have a whole wall in one room with nothing but extra books on the shelves, and I've heard high school students say that you have to read them and give book reports. I know I'll have to study more there and take books home, but it's going to be exciting with different teachers for each class and different rooms. They have five or six different rooms there. The agriculture room is in the basement, and it has a shop next to it. All the boys take agriculture, and I'll get to join the F. F. A. and get a pretty blue jacket to wear. The best room is the big gym where we'll have basketball practice the last two periods of the day, and I can't wait.

When I get home from school and change to work clothes and go out to get the cows for milking time, it's a good feeling. I never mind too much going after the cows. If they're in a far field, I sometimes take Lady if my granddad isn't using her. Or I walk along and think and dream a little. In the fall, it's nice and cool and clear and some of the days are almost perfect. The grass has stopped growing and has been trimmed down by the mowing and the grazing. It makes the fields smoother and cleaner looking. The trees are turning and you can see the squirrels running about and can spot them in the big oaks and hickory trees quicker as the leaves slowly begin to turn and fall. Everything seems to take on an easier way.

The cows move along better going to the barn in the cooler days. They don't stay around the shade as much and are glad to meander to the barn to get their bags emptied. The flies and the heat of the summer make them a little contrary at times, and they don't drive as easy in the heat. If I'm on Lady, she knows how to stay behind them and actually stops if a cow stops. She even moves over behind a contrary cow without my having to guide her there. She does the same thing with the sheep, but driving in sheep is a little different than driving in cows. Sheep stay closer together, but cows spread out more. The best way for both is to go easy once you get them moving. You have to know their ways, and talk to them to settle them. My granddad sure knows how to talk to his sheep. They know his voice when he rides out and begins calling them "Sheepy, oh, sheepy, sheepy, come sheepy." Most of the time, they'll come to him. They won't listen to me as well, but it's probably because I'm not as interested as he is.

The weather from mid-September to mid-October is the best of all. Each day gets a little cooler, and the color of everything begins to stand out. The air gets cleaner and clearer as the heat weakens and the hot summer winds die out. The stormy, unsettling days are over, and the hills quiet down like they are getting ready for sleep. Everything just seems more peaceful in the fall when I'm back on a ridge by myself with the cows and headed for the barn. All the hard work of planting and growing and harvesting is over. Everything was happening so fast that you couldn't keep up. And now it's like the earth and the woods and the fields are beginning to reach out for a pretty quilt and to tuck in for a night of rest and quiet peaceful dreams.

I know I don't explain everything the way it really is, or the feelings that seem to change along with the seasons. Clear cooler days make me feel better, and I don't have to think as much about wishing I could sit under a shade tree to get away from the sweat bees and the hot sun. In the summer with a field full of mown hay, I can't stop and take in all that is around me. There is so much to do to just keep up. But as the days cool down and the work slows down some, it's like the cooler, clearer days are coming along to give me more time to think and look all around at what nature is doing.

My mind changes along with nature's change. I have to change from thinking about the farm work to school work, and then when I get home from school, I have to change back into work clothes and head for a field or to a woods where Crit and Sollie might be building fence or cutting winter wood. In a way, I don't like to change from good school clothes to work clothes, because it's back to work again. But it does give me a free feeling to walk down the ridge and just be away to myself. The farm lets me be away where I can get that free feeling, and not be penned in where I feel like I can't get out. I can get to thinking more about myself and how I kind of join in with all that is around me. Walking down the ridge to help Crit and Sollie at the woods, or driving the cows to the barn in the bright, cool fall air makes me feel like I'm not scared of the future. It's a time when I seem to know that everything is settling down, and good feelings overtake anything that makes me feel a little scary about things.

Usually, I can get in a couple hours work after school before milking time. My granddad always tells me in the morning what to do when I get home. Building or fixing fence is a fall job when things slow down, but we have to fix fence whenever the cows or sheep break through at any time of the year. We always try to put up a new fence whenever one gets so old and rusty that it isn't much good anymore. Digging post holes for the locust posts is the hardest part, especially in ground that is very rocky. We cut and use locust posts, because they last for many, many years. It is sure hard on your arms to dig post holes, but I had to start doing it when I got big enough. I had to learn how to handle barbed wire when we were stringing it along the top of a woven-wire fence or patching up a weak part of an older fence.

Farmer's hands stay tough, because they have to handle about every thing that sticks in your skin. Briars, thorns, barbed wire and rough, sharp rocks keep your hands cut and scraped, and splinters and thorns are always getting stuck in your fingers. Whenever you get a big old splinter in a finger, you take the sharp point of your pocketknife blade and dig it out and go on. When you think about it, your hands do most everything in farming. My hands soften up as the school year goes along, and I have to toughen them up again each spring. But they never get as tough as the hands of our tenants and hired hands. My granddad has the toughest hands of all. He can handle about anything and never seems to let it bother him.

The fall of the year is the best time to get in winter wood. A long cold winter uses up a lot of cooking and heating wood. The tenants have to keep a little wood at the house year around for the cook stove. My mother used to use a wood cook stove, and then we got a kerosene cook stove when I was about six, and it was easier for her and didn't heat up the kitchen as much. We've had an electric stove for cooking for about a year now, and it's much cleaner and better for her.

We used to burn only wood for heating. The way our house is built is that on one side we have the kitchen in the back and the living room in the front. In between is the dining room, which we don't use much in the winter. We seldom heat anything except the kitchen and the living room, so to go from the kitchen to the living room, you have to go through a cold dining room. But new things are coming along all the time to make it better. We got a big Warm Morning stove for the living room, and it holds heat almost all the night through. We started burning coal in it, which is warmer and better. Trucks from down in the mountains come up with loads of coal and sell it to people who can afford something better than wood, which doesn't cost anything but a lot of chopping and hauling. I only have to carry in about two buckets of coal each day for the living room stove. We used to use the big fireplace in the kitchen to heat the kitchen, but now we have a little sheet-iron stove for wood, and it heats up real good. I sure liked to watch the big fire burn in the fireplace. Coming in from the barn on a cold winter day, I'd just stand there in front of the fire for a long time and let it warm me. After standing there for a while and watching the red, orange, yellow and blue flames dance about, it kind of drew me in with it, and it was like a long story that kept being told. It made me forget the cold and the mud and snow and the work. It was always a good warm story, and my mind could play along with the flames and reach up like they did. It was like reaching for something that was good and knowing that I could have it.

To gather in winter wood, you have to go cut trees or use those that have fallen from a storm or old age or disease. The tenants have to get in a lot of winter wood, for heating and cooking. A man with a sharp ax can chop up a lot of wood in a day, but it's hard to hit the blade into the wood at the right place every time. Some men can hit it right most every time, and some can't. Hitting the wood in the right place will bring a tree down pretty quick if the blade is razor sharp. And you have to know how to chop so that you can drop a tree in the right place. You don't want it to fall just anywhere, because it might get lodged against another tree or fall over a fence. Chopping is hard work, and you get a break whenever you need to sit down and file the blade as sharp as a razor. It's important to keep all work tools sharp, and you have to know how to sharpen everything. That way, it makes hoeing and chopping and mowing much easier and better.

I've used an ax for some time now, but my mother was always afraid for me to use one, especially when I was younger. I have to split up wood so it will fit in the stove before I carry it in to the back porch. I still can't chop down a tree too good, but hope to be able to do it like a man someday soon. It's hard to do, and sometimes I pretend that I'm swinging a bat in a baseball game. But when that happens, I usually don't do it well, because my mind wanders. My granddad has always said that you can't let your mind wander and work at the same time.

I'm now big enough to help use a crosscut saw. One of the hardest things to do is sawing with a two-man crosscut saw, and I never want to have to use one for very long. Whenever we have a big tree to cut, we saw it rather than using an ax. A crosscut saw is a sharp-toothed blade about six or seven feet long with two wooden handles on each end. One man gets on one end and one on another, and it's back and forth, back and forth, pushing, pulling, pushing and pulling. When we cut a big tree down next to the ground, you have to get down on your knees and sideways and push, pull, push, pull. You have to move it back and forth in a smooth way and work together, or the saw won't cut through the wood right.

After we've cut down enough trees and then cut them up into long poles about 12 feet long, we haul or drag them in with the horses, and wait for a neighbor to come to saw them up. It would take too long to cut up each piece of firewood, but that's the way we used to do it. One of the neighbors has a big saw blade mounted on the front of his tractor. He comes and the saw spins around real fast off a big belt hooked to the tractor motor. We then lift the long poles of wood up to the saw, and it cuts up the firewood real fast into chunks for the stove.

A big pile of cut up firewood looks mighty good when you're all finished. It's like so many things on the farm. You work hard to do something, and then it's a good feeling knowing the house will stay warm all winter.

Whether it's sawing or chopping or anything on the farm, you have to learn how to do everything the right way to get anything done. It's like spelling and arithmetic in school. It's either right or wrong, and my granddad always says you have to learn how to do it the right way. He looks around at other farmers and sees them fiddling around too much, because they don't do things the right way. And most of our tenants know how to use an ax or a plow or anything and they are pretty smart in their way. It goes to show that there are two kinds of learning. School, which is mostly using your mind, and farming, which is mostly using your back and arms and hands. You sure have to use your legs in plowing or forking hay up on a wagon all day. My legs have gone up and down our hills many times when my granddad has me go to a hollow or the bushes after a stray sheep or cow. I go after the horses every morning and the cows at night, and it's funny, though, how my legs get tired just sitting at a school desk all day.

It's different to go from one to the other. When I get home from school and change into work clothes, it feels good to head back the ridge and be out and away from lessons. It frees up my mind. I don't have to memorize poems or keep my papers neat and clean. In school, you aren't free. It's interesting to learn some of the things there, and when we get to play basketball, it kind of keeps us going. Most of the boys don't see how books help you to do things like chop wood or hoe tobacco. They sure have a hard time to come right out of milking in the morning and go straight to a desk seat in school for all day.

I can see how both could work out. I know that if I want to really go on and maybe be a lawyer or something, then I'll have to get my mind away from just walking down the ridge and having that free feeling. I do like learning about some of the history and our presidents. It's interesting to see how they figured out so many things for our country. My granddad says that many of them were lawyers and that most politicians are lawyers. I think he would like me to be a lawyer, but he's never said. He always likes to talk to people when he can about the president and our government and what they're doing. When he comes back from the legislature, he really likes to talk about what they did. He can't talk much to our tenants and hired hands, because they don't know much about what is going on with the government, but he likes to talk to the men about our laws during the Sunday School lesson and after church out in the yard. At Sunday School, the men get off on politics and away from Bible lessons and sometimes get pretty loud, because I can hear them.

I don't know whether it's best to think about keep going on to school and then to college, or to just stay on the farm and finally be

132

my own boss and not be tied up sitting like I do when at school. It gets pretty tiring, and being cooped up like chickens in a pen might be hard to do. It's like when I go see my real dad.

I haven't told you about my real dad, because I don't see him much. He is kind of like one of my uncles, but I see some of my uncles more then I do my real dad. My mother and real dad divorced when I was about two or three. Sometimes I think I remember it, but I'm not sure if I do or not. My real dad moved away to Lexington, Kentucky, which is a city and not a town. They have swimming pools and five picture shows there. He drives a Greyhound bus as his job and he got married again. Her name is Jelemma, and she treats me and my sister good whenever we go see them. His name is Leland, but everybody calls him Country. He said he got that name when he moved to town when he was young.

We go see them three or four times a year. In the summer, we go and spend about a week with them. It sure is different there in the city. They treat us nice, and we get to go swim in real swimming pools and go to picture shows and eat sometimes in restaurants. And we get an ice cream cone nearly every day. You can walk right up the street to a store, and it's easy to get soft drinks and everything.

It's always fun to go visit them with everything so different. They have a bathroom and a furnace in the basement so they don't have to carry in wood. We take a bath nearly every day there and always wear good clothes. I never have to do any real work there. I do mow the yard, but that's nothing, because yards in a city are so small. And I help wash their car and dry dishes, but that doesn't take long. We play games and play with some neighbor kids, but the big difference is not having to go to the field or the barn. You sit around the house and keep everything clean, and as I've gotten older, I've started feeling cramped up. You can walk down the street, but you can't walk anywhere to get away from everybody. People are all around you all the time.

It's funny in a way. When I'm alone somewhere back a ridge on the farm, I think about wishing I were with people so I could talk and have fun. But just being around people all the time at Lexington, I start feeling like there's no other place to go. Wearing good, clean clothes all the time makes you feel like you're at church or school all the time. I like to feel free, where it doesn't matter if you get mud or even a little cow manure splattered on you. I don't know if I want to be cramped up when I have to decide what to do when I leave home.

A city or town is exciting with so many things that make your life easier. All the picture shows and stores are right there, and you don't have to wonder if you'll get to go to town on Saturday when you're out forking hay on a hot day. But I don't know if I like buildings and streets and people all around more than I like to go out to the barn or head for the woods and just be able to think without being bothered with anything.

My real dad doesn't seem like a real dad. I don't know what he seems like. He is always nice and gives me presents at Christmas, but he kind of seems far away. My granddad seems more like a real dad in a way. I'm not sure what a real dad is supposed to be. There's not much else to explain about my real dad, because he's not around me much. He doesn't tell me what to do, and doesn't talk to me all that much whenever I see him. His life is different from mine, and it may be because he's used to the city and I'm not. I feel a little tight around him, and sometimes don't know what to say to him, and he acts like he doesn't know what to say to me. It confuses me some, but it doesn't bother me, because I don't try to figure it out.

It's hard to figure a lot of things out. I used to think I never wanted to be a farmer, because of all the hard work. I love to go to a town or city, but don't feel free and easy there like I do at home. Maybe I could get used to it, but I don't know.

I do know that one of the big days is when we fill silo. When the silage corn stalks and leaves have dried out and turned to a light brownish tan in late October, it's time to fill the silo. Our silo is made out of thick tile and is about 40 feet tall. There is nothing that smells any better than fresh silage, and the cows eat it like I eat ice cream whenever we make a freezer full on Sundays in the summer.

My granddad lets me stay home from school on silo-filling day, and it's a big day for me. The main reason it's so much fun is that about ten of our neighbors gather in with their teams of horses and wagons to help, and their wives gather in to help cook the big dinner. Silo filling in our neighborhood is spread out so each farmer can help the other ones fill theirs. Another reason I like this day is that we get a man who has a big red Farmall tractor and a silage cutter to come the night before and set up everything so that the next morning we can start early. I like to watch the big tractor start up with all its power, and if I ever decide to farm when I get older, I'll get a tractor the first thing.

To fill a silo, you have to first grow the corn, and it takes about ten acres to have enough, and it takes a lot of work with all the plowing, disking and planting in the spring. There are actually three types of corn that we grow. One is the corn we grow in the garden for roasting ears to eat and can for the winter. Another is field corn or horse corn as we call it, and it grows good, big long ears for the horses, cows, chickens and sheep. You can also eat it, but it is not as sweet as what we grow in the garden. In the winter, we grind up some of these big ears for the cows and give them a half-gallon bucket full over their scoop of silage. They go after it like it's icing on a cake, and it makes them give a lot more milk. When they're working hard, the horses also get a few ears at dinnertime. It doesn't have to be crushed for them, because they pick every kernel from the cob and it gives them strength. In the winter when the sheep are lambing, they need a little crushed corn each day so they have plenty of milk for their lambs. The chickens come running every time I go towards the corncrib. I like to take an ear or two, shell it with my hands and throw it down on the ground for them. They get right up to my feet and gobble the kernels up whole. Silage corn grows tall with big long leaves and does not have as big an ear as horse corn.

Well, in the fall when the corn has dried out and is ready, you have to start several days ahead to cut off the stalks at the ground with a long corn knife and put it in piles. Our farm hands wear long sleeves when they cut the corn, because the dried corn leaves get pretty sharp and can scratch your arms like you ran them through a briar patch. I'm in school when we cut corn, so I've never had to cut too much of it. It's not as hard as cutting tobacco, but it's still hard like most everything else.

On silo-filling day early in the morning, I can hear the neighbor farmers coming up the pike with their teams and wagons, and can hear the iron-rimmed wheels rolling along the road for a mile or two away in the quiet crisp morning air. It's usually a beautiful fall day, and you know that it will be a long and hard day. But the farmers all seem to like to do it, because it gives them a chance to work together

135

and talk and visit and help out their neighbors. The women all pitch in and talk and laugh and make as big and as good a dinner as they can.

The wagons then head to the field to load the piles of corn, and then take the big loads to the barn. The big tractor starts up, and two men start feeding the long corn stalks in to the silage cutter. The tractor makes a lot of noise as it turns the cutter real fast with a long thick leather belt running from a fly wheel on the tractor to the cutter. It turns so fast that it cuts up the corn into little slivers and blows it all the way up a pipe to the top of the silo. The fresh moist silage then falls down into the silo. This goes on all day long until the silo is full.

When it's dinnertime, the tractor shuts off and the farmers gather in the backyard at the cistern to wash up for dinner. I know my mother worries about having a good dinner, but all the women helping seem to know how to make everything work out. They set bowl after bowl of beans and potatoes and corn and everything out and a big roast with biscuits and gravy. They just keep bringing food out to the back porch, and when the men are eating so much, it's like the women know that the men know it's good. At the end, they bring out big apple cobblers and pumpkin and cushaw pies with fresh whipped cream to go on top. When dinner is over the farmers go lie down in the backyard and light up a smoke or put in a chew and just lie there and talk and laugh for a few minutes until the tractor starts up again.

I like this day, because I like to watch the neighbors and their teams of horses, and I like to hear them talk, and I like most of all to watch and listen to the tractor. Sometimes my granddad will tell me to go into the silo to help stomp the silage down to keep it even. We always have one man in there to guide the inside pipe around so the silage stays level and doesn't pile up. I don't like to do this because of all the interesting things outside. My granddad must know how much I like silo-filling day, because he lets me wander around and watch more than he makes me help out. He understands some things about me sometimes just when I think he never does.

# CHAPTER TEN

## WHEN THE DEW TURNS TO FROST

I don't know how much my granddad understands me, or if he really tries to. It seems more and more that I don't want to go along with him as much. When I get to feeling disgusted with him when he keeps telling me to do everything, he'll ease up and do something for me like letting me go easy on silo-filling day. He does know how to get the most out of our tenants and other hired hands, and he gets them to work in a peaceful way most of the time, and they like him. From what I can tell, the neighbors and the preacher like him a lot and ask him advice. The people in town where he goes to meetings about farming and other things call him often to talk to him about certain things. He talks to people about what they do in the legislature. You can tell he feels the legislature is very important, but I don't really know what they do up there. He's kind of up in the world in a way, but doesn't act like he's a big shot like some high-up government people do.

Although he has to go off to the capitol in Frankfort for a few weeks, we still do most everything on the farm in an old-fashioned way. As I get older, I think I would rather be like Leslie Warren with the big tractor and silage cutter than the farmers with the team of horses and wagons who have to do the hard part. I want to decide some things by myself. And it seems like as I get older, my granddad expects more and more out of me. I don't get disgusted too much, though, because I know he really wants me to get an education and go up in the world. He can be hard, but I think he believes everything will work out for me in a good way, and this kind of keeps me going.

You can tell he has a good feeling when the silo is full and the hay loft is full and there are extra tall stacks of hay out on the tops of ridges. And he always makes sure there is plenty of the best alfalfa to winter our sheep. With the tobacco barns full of curing stalks, and the wood house full of cut wood chunks and the corn crib soon to be full of long yellow ears, there are other things to gather before the frost comes. As I said, you put everything out in the spring and then bring it all in during the fall.

I have to go gather several baskets full of hickory nuts and walnuts to store for the winter. There are two kinds of hickory nuts, the big kind and the small kind, which is a little bigger than a marble. The shagbark hickory trees grow the big kind, and they are good too, but the small kind is better to eat. My mother likes the smaller ones to put in candy and cakes. When the hickory nuts begin to fall, you have to beat the squirrels to them and find them mixed in with the fallen leaves under the trees. I told you about the time when my granddad whipped me a little with a switch when I lied to him about hulling all the walnuts. I'll always remember that, but now I know how to hull walnuts without getting the stain all over me and it doesn't bother me. Walnuts are very good in candy and cakes, or you can just eat the big kernels by themselves.

After most everything has ripened in the fall, we like to eat persimmons, paw-paws and haws that grow back on the place. We don't plant these trees. They just grow wild on their own. Of course, you can't eat persimmons until after a frost, because a green persimmon will turn your mouth inside out. Paw-paws grow in little patches down next to creeks. Not many city people even know what a paw-paw is, but if they're good and soft and ripe, they taste something like a banana and even look something like a banana, being long and yellow.

It's funny how nature works. Some years, the hickory nut crop isn't too good and some years there aren't any paw-paws at all. About once every five years, the hawthorn trees bear fruit. You can't eat much of a haw, because it is a little red thing smaller than a hulled walnut. It looks like a little apple and tastes something like a very sweet apple. The years that we have them, I pick a pocket full on the way to get the cows, and get a few good bites on the way.

Some years we raise cane for sorghum and some years we don't. In the late fall, my granddad always likes his fresh sorghum molasses on his biscuits, and my mother uses it to make popcorn balls. They are the best things. She knows just how to heat up the sorghum enough to mix it with popcorn and make it into a ball, and after supper before we go to bed, we eat one and sometimes she'll pack one in my lunch for school. She makes molasses candy, which is so good. She boils a big batch until it gets like a sticky ball and then starts pulling at it until it gets lighter and softer. After it is not too sticky and a little bit hard, she cuts it into pieces and we have molasses candy.

In the years that we don't grow cane, my granddad buys a gallon bucket or two of fresh-made sorghum. When we raise sorghum cane, we cut the stalks off in the field, strip off the leaves and take a wagon load of the stalks a couple of miles up to Warny Hopkin's place back at the end of Slick Ridge where he makes the sorghum. He knows how to boil the juice just right to get sorghum that is not too sweet, but doesn't have a bitter twang to it. The first fresh batch in the fall is mighty good. It seems like everything comes on at the right time. There is nothing better than the first strawberries in May, and new sorghum in the fall is about as good.

We never had beehives for honey, but some of the neighbors do. We buy a quart jar or two from them, or they'll give us a jar. We have found beehives in the cracks of hollow trees, and we've had tenants who got the honey out, but my granddad never fools with bees. You can't do everything. Some of the good neighbors give us things we don't have, like honey or certain kinds of apples, and we give them stuff from our garden if they don't have any. It works out to help each other, and most of our neighbors act real friendly with us. My granddad says that if you're ever in a pinch, you need good neighbors.

My mother thinks I eat too much for my size, and my granddad and uncles, whenever they come, laugh about all that I eat. I guess I need all of it to grow. When you're out running sheep and cows up and down hills or milking late, you can get real hungry. When my mother goes to town to the grocery, she sometimes hides the good things from me. One day last winter, she came home with a dozen oranges, and I ate most of them in two days. I don't know why oranges taste so good to me in the winter.

We get to eat a lot of different things at our school's Halloween party every year. The Halloween party is the one time of the year when most everybody goes to the school and takes their kids. They have all kinds of games and booths and chili and many other things to eat. And usually they have some fiddle and guitar music, and then toward the end, they have a contest for the best costume for the kids and for the older people. It's fun when everybody takes their masks off, because you don't know who everybody is when they're all dressed up going around scaring the little kids. It's a big night, and it used to scare me some when bigger people dressed up real scary, but now I hang around the older boys and the high school boys who come and talk about playing tricks on people.

The older boys go out and drive around and do things to people's barns or yards. They'll stack pumpkins in the road or move a woodpile up around a back porch if they know all the family is at the Halloween party. One of my uncles told me that once when he was young, the boys put a wagon up on the neighbor's barn roof. I've heard that at town, the older boys stack up all kinds of things under the red light. They bring in old machinery, fodder shocks, pumpkins and junky stuff. The town police can't handle it all, so they give up. When the Halloween party is over and it's time to go home, you know your car windows are going to be soaped up. But the worst thing is that every year they turn over the outside toilets at school. Every year the day after, Miss Carrie takes each older boy into the office and asks him if he knows who did it. She never finds out, because we always say we don't know. I do not know, and I know I should tell if I did, but it would be hard to tell her. I never like to see people do bad things, but if one of your friends does a bad thing, it's hard to think what to tell about it.

One of the boys copies the answers to our math problems, and he gets 100's on his papers. My mother always told me to never copy, and the teachers always tell us the same. I can't tell on him, because most all the kids don't like a tattletale. It bothers me to see him get it all right, when I might miss some of the answers. Whenever I see him copy, I don't know what to do about it. If you tell on people for everything, nobody will like you. But if somebody did something really bad, I know I should tell. One time last year, our teacher took us for a walk through the woods by the school. A couple of big eighth graders stayed back to smoke. I saw them and they said if I told, they'd stomp my ass. I don't like to see people breaking the rules and getting away with it, but I guess you have to live with certain things that people do wrong, but I don't know why.

When Halloween is over and we get into November, the weather starts getting colder, and the first frost comes and most all the leaves have fallen. Work on the farm slacks off with the crops, and I don't have too much to do after school except get the cows and help milk. As the days get shorter, we milk earlier, and then have more time to

140

sit around the house at night. Of course, Crit and Sollie are doing something every day like patching fence, hauling rock or cleaning up ground. They also have a little time to squirrel hunt, and the hunting season for rabbits and quail in the winter is coming on.

Most all men who live on farms have guns and hunt. You have to have guns to kill varmints or dogs in the sheep and for hunting. My granddad has two shotguns and two rifles. He liked to bird hunt most of all, but with his bad joints and arthritis it's harder for him to walk up and down the hills. That's why he rides Lady most everywhere. But he likes to talk about his hunting days and how good a shot he was. He has always let me be around guns and shoot them. I've been hunting with my uncles and once in awhile with a tenant. Some of the boys at school hunt whenever they can, because they like to kill things.

I guess it's no different in fishing, because you kill a fish if you clean it. It seems different in killing a rabbit or a pretty squirrel. I don't get to go fishing that much unless an uncle takes me over to Fork Lick Creek or the South Licking River about once a summer. We do have some bream and bluegill in some of our ponds, and I go fish one of the ponds some. When I hook a pretty bluegill and pull it out and it flops all over the bank fighting for its life, I think about not wanting to scrape the scales and cut its head off and cut out its guts. But I know I'll have to get used to it and not keep on being babified.

I like hunting some, but not all that much, and I can do it or not do it. I don't know what it is, but to shoot a pretty red-fox squirrel out of a tree and see it drop down on the ground all bloody bothers me some like seeing a fish flop around the bank. I know boys who will shoot at most anything. Now I know that squirrels, rabbits and birds provide meat, and we like to have a good mess of any of them now and then. A big skillet of young squirrel or rabbit fried up golden brown tastes good after eating so much fried chicken, cured pork meat, or lamb or beef roasts. A young squirrel or rabbit is much more tender and better than a tough old one, and the white gravy made from the drippings of either is the best gravy of all. A quail breast is maybe the best meat of anything. You get two pieces of meat from a quail. One piece is mostly all a pure white breast, and the other piece is just a little piece of the back and two legs attached, which gives you about two good bites, but it's very good too. A quail has a little pulley bone in the breast like a chicken. When I was little, my sister and I would make a wish and then pull on the pulley bone, and when it broke, the one who got the largest piece of the bone got their wish. The tenants hunt and eat game meat a lot more than we do, because they don't have as much other kind of meat. But just to go out and kill anything for fun bothers me more than it used to.

I did something a while back that really made me feel bad. Sometimes after school when I go after the cows, I take my 22 rifle in case I see something. Well, I was walking along a hollow and heard a noise way up in a tree. I could only see a little fur ball up through the leaves, but I aimed and fired. I thought it must be a squirrel, but two little things fell to the ground, and I had knocked two baby coons out of the tree. It surprised me, and one kept crying and shaking about on the ground. The other had been hit with the bullet and was dead. But the live one kept crying and probably screaming for its mother. I thought what had I done. They were actually cute little things and the crying and struggling of the live one kept bothering me, and I didn't know what to do. I wanted to take it all back, but I knew I couldn't let the little hurt one just stay there in pain, so I aimed and fired another bullet through its head and the crying and squirming stopped. I almost cried myself, and wondered why I shot for no good reason. Sometimes my mind goes back to that crying little coon, and I still don't feel good.

It will soon be hog killing time, and I'll watch Crit take his 22 and hit the fatting hogs right between the eyes and watch them drop and squeal. Then one of the other men will rush up and stick a sharp butcher knife in the hog's throat and jump back to get away from the stream of hot blood squirting out. The men go right on and talk about making sure the shooter hits the hog in the right spot, and they act like seeing a hog or anything drop is nothing. I don't know if I will ever be able to shoot a hog or a beef between the eyes when they're just standing there looking at me, but I know I'll have to show everybody that I am not afraid to kill one when the time comes.

I've told you about when I killed a dog that was in the sheep, but would you rather have a wild curry dog dead or several of your sheep mangled or dead? One day last winter, I got into killing something that I still think about, and sure wish that I hadn't come across it that way. It was a big red fox, and I killed it because I thought I had to.

The way it went was that my granddad sent me to our far barn at what we always called the other place. Every two or three days he would go over or send me over to throw down some hay from the loft for the cattle or sheep that we might have over there. He had noticed that a den of foxes was getting pretty thick over there. Too many foxes can become a nuisance, so he set out a couple of steel traps near their den down the hill below the barn. When I got to the barn, I looked down the hill and saw a big fox in one of the traps jumping around trying to get away. I went down and the fox started jumping around even more when I got up to him. When an animal steps on a steel trap, the clamps that spring closed will hold the leg of something as big as a very big strong dog.

I thought what was I going to do. It had gnawed on its leg trying to get away. The leg was bloody and looked awful. It kind of made me sick. The fox kept struggling to get away, but the steel trap wouldn't let go. I had no gun, but knew I had to kill it to get it out of its misery. I picked up a tree limb and broke it off to make a club. The first hit at its head has to be a good one. If you stun an animal at first, then you can kill it with several more blows. It was very hard for me to make the first good hit, but I knew I had to do it. It went down and then I made several more good blows to make sure it was dead. I was so nervous and weakly. And it all got me to thinking that I don't know if I ever want to kill anything ever again. I don't know why we have to step in and do hard things when we don't want to.

We don't have to work on Thanksgiving afternoon, because we always go hunting on that day. Hunting doesn't seem as bad when you kill something as it did when I killed the fox. But Thanksgiving is a pretty big day. At school, all the little kids color papers with turkeys, leaves and Pilgrims and they are put up on the walls and it becomes real colorful and reminds us to be thankful. It all reminds us that it won't be long until Christmas comes, which is the biggest day of the year.

We usually begin stripping tobacco along about Thanksgiving, and we usually strip tobacco Thanksgiving morning and then go to the house for the big dinner. Some of my uncles, aunts and their kids come for the dinner, and my mother cooks about everything. We've never raised turkeys, but some of the neighbors do, and we usually get one from them. The best thing about the Thanksgiving dinner is all the dressing and fresh rolls and mashed potatoes with the giblet gravy. You put the gravy over the dressing and rolls and potatoes and you're sure ready for the afternoon hunt. My mother buys cranberries for Thanksgiving, but I never could see why it made the dinner any better. She also buys a few oysters and makes oyster dressing out of crackers, butter and milk, and it is so good. When you eat dressing of every kind, it stuffs you full. Of course, we finish with pumpkin and cushaw pies with fresh whipped cream, and are then ready to go get some rabbits and birds.

The day after Thanksgiving, we're back in the stripping room. Some farmers have their stripping room out alongside their tobacco barn and some have it built in a corner of their barn. Ours is in a corner, and we spend many winter days in there stripping the leaves from the tobacco stalks. A stripping room is about the size of a living room in a house. It has windows across one side so you can see the leaves real well and know which leaves to pull and to tie into hands. A hand is what farmers call a hand full of stripped leaves. The stripping room has a bench running all down the side under the windows, which is where the stalks are laid while stripping them. The room also has a chimney and a little wood stove to keep you warm while you're just standing there day after day on cold winter days.

Before stripping can start, the tobacco has to be cured up good and brown. Before it can be taken down from the rails in the barn, it has to come in case. Case means that it gets moist and will not crumble up when you start handling it. Of course, the tobacco gets very dry hanging up there, and it takes a good rain or fog to bring it in case so it can be taken down and piled into bulks. Some years, late fall is very dry, and you have to wait for rain and moisture to bring the tobacco in case. All farmers hope for some rain around Thanksgiving so they can start stripping and have some of their tobacco to sell before Christmas. It sure makes a good Christmas if there's some money coming in at that time.

I usually go to the stripping room after school and help out until it gets too dark to pick out and pull the different colored leaves from the stalks. I always have to help out with stripping on Saturdays and when we're off school for Christmas. It gets tiring to just stand there by the bench and do nothing but strip the leaves all day, but it's warm by the fire and we can talk and tell jokes and laugh some. My granddad doesn't want us to talk and laugh too much, because he says you can't keep your mind on what you're doing.

He knows it's very important to strip the right colored leaves and separate them and not mix them up. The reason it is so important is that you get different prices for different grades of tobacco. The way it works is that a stalk has about five or six grades of tobacco on it. Down next to where you have cut the stalk off near the ground are a few leaves of what is called trash. As you go up the stalk, you get flyings, lugs, red and tips at the top end. Flyings might bring 45 cents a pound, lugs about 40 cents a pound, red leaves only about 30 cents a pound and tips even less. So you want to have a good crop with a lot of the good leaves, and you don't want to mix up the leaves in the hands, because the buyers don't want it that way, and you won't get a good price.

The good trash and lug leaves go into the good cigarettes like Camels, Lucky Strikes and Phillip Morris. Buffalo and Bull Durham, which you have to roll on your own, does not take the best tobacco leaves and is cheaper than a pack of Camels or Chesterfields. Tenants and hired hands usually smoke roll-your-own and some of them can roll a cigarette to where it looks real nice. The best lug leaves go into cigars, but not too many farmers will smoke a cigar unless it's on a Sunday when they're sitting around in the shade and talking with visitors. I'm not sure what goes into pipe tobacco, but it is mixed together, and one can of pipe tobacco must be different from the other. My granddad used to always smoke Granger pipe tobacco, but he's gotten away from it some, because it bothers his throat. My real dad whenever I go see him smokes Velvet in his pipe. Some people like one kind and some another. It's like which kind of ice cream you like, or which kind of candy bar or a Coke or Pepsi or orange.

It seems that the more money you have tells whether you smoke or chew. Many tenants and hired hands chew, and some chew plug, some chew twist and some chew scrap. Day's Work, Brown Mule and Star are the best plugs. Wild Duck is a good twist and Beech Nut or Mail Pouch are scrap tobacco that most chew. I don't plan to smoke or chew mainly because I know that basketball players are not supposed to smoke, because it takes your wind. But I've tried some of it when I was younger. When you take a big bite out of a Brown Mule plug, you start spitting like crazy. It's real powerful and it made me a little dizzy when I once tried it.

So you stand there day after day and try to strip the right leaves to get the best price. A big armload is brought in from the bulk in the barn and put on the bench. The first man pulls off the flyings and then passes the stalk to the next man, who pulls the trash, and then the next man, who strips the lugs, and on and on. Kids usually strip the tips so they don't mix up the good leaves. When you get a hand full of leaves, you wrap another leaf real tight around the hand and then put it on a tobacco stick. When a stick gets full with about 18 hands, it's put in a wooden press and tightened down so the tobacco is packed real good. The pretty packed hands are stacked in a nice even bulk out in the barn and covered with a tarpaulin to keep them moist. Then the tobacco is ready to be loaded on a truck and taken to the sales. When that day comes, you want to make sure you've done all that you could have done with your crop. Making all the payments at the end of the year depends on the crop. It's always sad to see a farmer work and worry with the crop and then have it do poorly at the sales. Many a farmer has had to go try to get a job on the highway or the railroad because of a poor crop year.

My granddad kind of hurries with many things he does, but he always wants us to baby the tobacco when it comes time to strip. We actually began the tobacco crop back in February when the plant beds were burned and sowed. We've stayed with it all year long and worried about it and planted it and plowed it and watched it. Now it's getting down to the end and a whole year's work will either turn out good or not so good.

I'm pretty good with knowing the different tobacco grades now, and seldom put a red leaf in a hand of lugs. Crit has bragged on me about it, and it makes me feel good to ever have anyone brag on me. Sometimes when I'm stripping and we're not talking and laughing, I get to thinking and dreaming. I don't know why I dream so much about people bragging on me. Whenever anyone does, it gives me an extra feeling. Most of the time, I dream about if I will be a star on Morgan's basketball team. When the people cheer after I hit a long one, it will give a feeling much bigger than having someone brag on me for knowing how to grade tobacco.

My granddad doesn't brag on me much about anything, and I don't know if he thinks I'm doing good or not. Oh, he'll let me know if I mess up or fool around too much. I most usually want to do a good job with whatever I'm doing, but sometimes I never know if it makes much of a difference except to keep out of trouble. At school, Miss Carrie will kind of brag on who makes 100s and put their papers up on the wall, but some kids can't do much of anything. It's usually the tenant kids who don't have good clothes and who never bring any store-bought things in their lunches, and I feel sorry for some of them. Most of them will never go on to high school or maybe only for one year or so. They probably never have anyone brag on them for anything, and that might keep them down.

Most of the time, I don't think about much else except myself. Like when you're younger, you don't notice much around you, but as I get older, I've noticed that I'm wondering more about why our life is the way it is. I never thought much about why the tenant kids never have much of anything, but now I wonder about it more. For a long time, I've wanted people to brag on me, but when they don't I just have to go on. I once thought about what if no one ever brags on you. What do you do?

All our preachers have preached that all you have to do is just turn your whole life over to God and Jesus. They will take care of you and not let you go to hell. Well, I don't know. I wonder why they take care of some of us more than others like the tenant kids, but I can't figure it out. Of course, I don't want to wind up in hell, so I try to be good, but I never know if God has ever bragged on me or not. I think that God has more power than Jesus, so I usually pray to him, and I try to be good, because I want him to let me be a star on Morgan's team. But I know that some of the best players there now smoke, drink, cuss and try to screw girls. So I wonder if God has it all planned out or not.

With winter coming on, we spend much more time at the barns, and they get to be more like another home again. In the summer, all the animals stay out in the field, and we use the barns only for milking, harnessing the horses, and putting up hay in the lofts. When the cold winds start blowing and the blustery clouds begin sprinkling down sleet and snow, the cows and the sheep need to stay in during the nights. There's always feeding to do and cleaning out the manure and throwing down hay and silage. With a month or more of bulking and stripping tobacco, we have to keep it all in order for the sheep and cows.

My granddad brings his sheep to a field closer to the barn when the cold nights come. The ewes wool coats have grown out thick and full by that time, and their bodies are full and round with one or two lambs inside soon ready to be born. He watches them closer then and can tell when they need a little hay or when they need to spend a blustery night in the barn. When the snows start blowing and the lambs start coming, he'll be with them off and on all through the days and nights.

Sometimes I think he pays more attention to his sheep than he does to me. Sometimes I think all he wants me to do is just work and do whatever he tells me. Sometimes I get tired of doing everything and wish that I were older and could be more of my own boss. And sometimes when I get to being a little disgusted with everything, he does something to change my mind. One day last summer, when we were out changing the sheep to a different pasture field, he told me that he would sell me five ewes and that I could start raising the lambs and get some money in the bank. He said that I could start paying for the five ewes when I sold their first lambs. He wrote down on paper that I owed him $200 and had me sign my name to it. I think he wanted to show me how he does it with the neighbors. With five ewes that we would pick out and mark with paint, I would be making clear money in a year or two.

He doesn't talk to me too much about important things or grown-up things, and I really didn't know why he did that at the time. But he said that I needed to know how to take care of money and write checks and save up for education or something. Well, it all surprised me and he kind of seemed glad about it. I could tell he thought I was getting to be more grown up, and needed to know how to watch everything closer and take hold of more things myself. It all made me take more of an interest, and then I didn't mind as much to go out on a cold, rainy on snowy day to bring the sheep to the barn. I started looking closer at all our sheep and always at my own ewes to see if they were doing all right. It all goes to show that he is pushing me into more man-like things, and it makes me feel that I can handle it.

The milking and the feeding and the stripping and everything comes first. But there has to be a way to take your mind off nothing but work. We boys finally got Miss Carrie to get us a basketball game with another school. Our county has three high schools, Butler, Falmouth and Morgan where I'll go, and they all have inside gyms. It also has seven grade schools up to the eighth grade. She finally called one of them a few weeks ago and the Mt. Auburn School said they would come over one afternoon and play the Goforth Green Devils. We were so excited about it, and I got my mother to cut out some green numbers to sew on our white undershirts so we would have part of a uniform. Some of our boys don't have tennis shoes. You can play outside with work shoes on about as well, but tennis shoes make you faster.

To get ready, we took some lime and put it down for lines on our outside basketball court. Miss Carrie asked one of the neighbor farmers who knew some of the rules to come and be the referee, and we were all set. Well, the Mt. Auburn Eagles loaded up their seventh and eighth grades in a school bus and came all the way across the county. It was a cool fall day and the wind was blowing a little, but you learn how to shoot with a wind, and we knew how our goals slanted so we won 30 to 10. It was a big day for our school. Miss Carrie said she would try to get us a game sometime in a real gym at night, and we are hoping it will be real soon. We're already talking about how we all can go to the game when it happens. Some of the boys are not sure if their daddies will take them or not.

Whenever I can, I go to the barn and practice shooting, but now that winter is coming on, the cold and the snow and the mud make it harder. I still go shoot and if it gets too cold, I even shoot with gloves on. I don't mind winter too much, because for one thing, we get to slide and skate around on the pond and sleigh ride down the hills in the snow. As the winter comes on, there are many days when it gets so bad you can't do too much on the farm except work around the barns feeding and straightening up.

My granddad sits around the house more when it starts getting cold. He's slowed down some, and doesn't like to go out in zero weather like he used to when it meant nothing to him. Some people start getting sadder in the wintertime. I guess it's because sitting by a fire so much gives you more time to think about everything. I know back during the war, people got more sad during the winter, waiting and wondering where their sons and husbands were and if they were wounded or killed in action. Sitting and waiting and wondering on dark cold days can give you bad feelings, and it was hard to have good feelings on cold winter days during the war. One thing to look forward to every day was the mail. If you got a letter, it helped out. Two of my uncles who were away in the war wrote us whenever they could. Writing was the only way to let anybody know what was going on. Soldiers said that if they weren't marching or fighting, writing a letter home took their minds off all their troubles. So people who never wrote much of anything started writing a lot. Some of the tenants, who could only read or write a little, would have somebody else write a letter for them to send to a relative in the war, and sometimes a soldier who didn't have much education would write a letter that you had trouble reading.

Whenever you went to the mailbox and had a letter from a soldier off in the war, you perked up. First of all, it told that the soldier was alive. My mother would read it and re-read it and then call my aunts and other kin and tell them all about what was in it. Once in a while, my uncles would write me a separate letter, and I was only about nine or ten at the time. My mother would tell me to write them back, which I would. I never knew much to tell them, but whenever I would do it, I would think about what if they were ever killed.

My Uncle John, who is my Aunt Fay's husband, was in Germany fighting against Hitler and the Nazis. He was the one who moved in with us to farm when the war broke out and they started drafting everybody to go fight. But he knew it was right to go fight, so he did. I remember how scary the name Nazis was, and you stayed scared of them and the way they looked with their salute to Hitler and the way they marched and looked so mean. The Japs were about as scary looking when you saw pictures of their snipers up in palm trees and shooting at us sneaky like. Their suicide bomber pilots that hit our ships were also very mean, and it was hard to understand why they wanted to kill us so much.

My Uncle John sent me through the mail a German helmet and a big long dagger that he captured. The helmet gave me the shivers. We would look at it and show it around and wonder how bad the man was who wore this helmet to give his life for Hitler.

But we don't think about the war that much anymore, and we don't have to worry whether our boys will ever get back home or not. Now Harry Truman says that we may have to go to war again against other bad countries. I've heard the preachers say many times that the Bible says there will be wars and rumors of war. I used to worry about it, but if I have to go when I'm older, I'll just go.

I say that we don't think about it much anymore, but then along about the time when the snows come and the dark days come and Christmas is coming, the people who lost their boys in the war start getting sad again. They know that it will be another Christmas without all of their family together. I've heard some women who lost husbands or sons say they don't know if they can bear another Christmas or not. Your family is the most important thing there is, and Christmas is a time that brings it all back together.

It's the biggest day of the year. I remember when I was a little boy and I could hardly wait until that morning. Once you get a week or so into December, the whole time is spent in thinking and getting ready for Christmas. I still get excited, but not like I used to. You still have work to do, and all the work seems like it finally leads up to Christmas, which is like ending a year before starting all over again.

As I've said before, the tobacco crop leads up to Christmas. All year long, you've done all you can do with it, and hope to have at least some of it ready for market before Christmas. If it is pretty good and brings a pretty good price, I guess that's the best Christmas present of all for a farmer. When the days and nights have cooled way down and stay that way around Thanksgiving time, it's time for hog-killing day. You're ready for some good fresh meat in December. But again, it's a day I never liked too much, because you see the hogs drop, and then scalded and cut up and the blood gets all over everything.

# CHAPTER ELEVEN
## WHEN EVERYTHING COMES TOGETHER

Crit is a good shot with a 22. On hog-killing day, we drive three or four good fat ones out to the lot by the chicken house to kill and butcher them. My granddad used to shoot them, but he lets Crit shoot them now, and he usually hits them in the right spot between the eyes so they drop and never know what hit them. I always have a bad feeling when they drop like that, but there's never much time to think about it, because another man rushes up and sticks a sharp butcher knife in their throat just in the right place. That's when the hot blood starts squirting all out, and if you're too close, it will spray on you or the wind can blow it on you. As a little kid, I kind of stayed away with all the blood and the guts and everything, but when you get old enough to help do anything, that's when you have to step in whether you want to or not.

It's a messy job and it stinks with the piss and shit coming out when a sharp knife blade cuts through the guts. You need three or four men to kill three or four hogs, and get them cut up by the end of the day. It takes a day or two more to work up all the meat, render the lard, grind the sausage and cure the side bacon, hams and shoulders.

You've fed the hogs corn and slop all summer and fall to get them fattened for good meat. Hogs aren't like cattle or sheep or horses. You never get to where they might seem like a friend in a way or where they seem to take much notice of you. You just don't seem to mind killing them as much as say killing a sheep or a beef. But after you see them lying there with all the blood drained out and ready for the scalding barrel, you still wish that nothing ever had to die.

A three-hundred-pound hog makes good meat. After the blood has drained out, the men rush in to drop the hog into a barrel of scalding water. We get the water boiling by building a big fire early in the morning and heating big rocks down in the hot coals. Then when it's time for the water to be heated, we shovel the rocks down in the barrel, and the water gets hot enough to scald the hog's tough thick hide. The men slosh the hog up and down in the barrel a few times to soften the hair. Now farmers have to know a lot, and they have to know just how hot to get the water and how many times to slosh the hog up and down and when to take it out and start scraping all the hair from the skin. If everything is not just right, it can singe and ruin the thick skin over the meat.

The weather has to be cold enough so that the meat won't spoil until it's worked up, salted and cured. But with a cold day, the big fire heating the rocks gives off some heat to keep you a little warm. Before too long, the men have blood, piss, water and other stuff on their clothes, and sloshing the hogs around in the hot water splatters some of it up and you have to be careful not to get scalded yourself. When the hogs are lifted out of the water, we scrape the hair all off with sharp butcher knives so the skin covering the hams, bacon and shoulders is smooth and clean for curing.

After all the hair is scraped off, we hang a hog up on a pole fixed for hanging three or four hogs, and somebody then slits all the way down the stomach and the guts fall out. I always stood back when this was going on, but now I have to step in. A boy gets the bad jobs sometimes, and my granddad told me to drag the guts to the hollow for the buzzards and dogs last year, and I now can help scrape the hogs too. I tell you, the first time you drag guts, you don't want to take hold, but if you stand back, then the men will think you're a sissy. The best way to do it is to jump right in, and if your clothes get all messy and wet, then it looks like you are as big as a man.

They cut off the head and saw down through the backbone. I don't know what it is, but when the head comes off, it gives me another funny feeling to see it lying there on the sled. You think back to just yesterday when you threw some ears of corn into the pen, and the hogs came running up and were glad you fed them and were happy. With their heads lying on the sled, you look at them and wonder if they maybe went to some place like a heaven or if there is nothing ever left of anything.

The men keep cutting up the parts and trimming, and then we take everything on the sled to the smokehouse. There we keep trimming and cutting. The fat pieces are cut up into small pieces and in a day or two, they'll be cooked down outside in a big iron kettle and made into lard. We get two or three four-gallon cans of lard to last for most of a year. The hams, shoulders and side pieces for bacon are trimmed up real good to be made ready for curing. A lot of scrap meat is trimmed off to be ground into sausage, and everybody likes a lot of good sausage seasoned with sage, salt and pepper.

After we get it all to the smokehouse, my granddad puts the hog heads up on the chopping block and I know he is going to tell me to go get a pan from the kitchen. He then takes a hatchet and splits open the skulls and dips out the brains. I'll take the pan of brains to the kitchen for tomorrow's breakfast. I don't know what it is, but seeing the brains gives me another funny feeling. You keep thinking about it all and the bad smells and your slimy clothes and the empty hog pen. When I go out by the hog pen that night, it seems kind of lonely.

There is so much to keep doing to finally get hog killing over. The loins have to be trimmed and the backbone and ribs trimmed, and we don't waste anything. My granddad says his dad always caught the blood in a bucket and they made blood pudding. We never do, and I don't think I could ever eat blood pudding. We do make cracklins from the skin covering the fat when the lard is cooked up and rendered. The cracklins are what's left of the skin when it has been boiled for several hours, and it is good to chew on. My granddad makes souse in a crock from some of the scrap pieces. It's something like sausage, but I don't eat much of it. My mother makes mincemeat from the meat scraps, and we eat a lot of mincemeat pies around Christmas time.

When you tell town people about butchering and eating hog brains and everything, they act funny about it and don't want you to keep talking about it. Some of the women can't stand to hear you tell about eating squirrel brains. Our first meal after hog killing is the brains. My mother fries them up mixed with scrambled eggs, and they are pretty good that way now. I used to keep thinking about the hogs wallowing around in the pen and then the guts falling out and everything, and I would have a hard time putting the fried brains in my mouth. You have to just go on and get used to everything that has to be done.

I think the reason my granddad makes me step in on hog killing and everything else now is that he knows I need to know how to do all kinds of work. He never says this is the way you are supposed to trim meat for sausage or this is the way to tie a sheep to shear it. He just tells me to be there and be ready to jump in and help when he thinks I'm old enough. When he wants me to jump in, I can't stand back.

You learn how to do different work because of watching it for many years. When you've had to go to the stripping room since you were little, you soon know a lug leaf from a red leaf. And there's something in you that wants to show big people you can do the hard things. One of our neighbors laughs about the time he came over to see my granddad about something and we were chopping the weeds out of a tobacco patch. He says that my granddad was going down a row chopping the weeds, and that I was very little, and also had a little hoe and was chopping along in the row behind him. The problem was that I was chopping down the tobacco plants. They all laugh about it now, but I always wanted to prove I was ready whether I was ready or not.

Learning to do everything is not like school learning. In school, we mostly read and write some things and take a test on it. But most of the kids don't pay much attention. Some of the dumbest kids in lessons are real good at hunting or trapping or doing hard work on the farm. One of the eighth grade boys has a hard time passing any lesson, but he works on their tractor better than his dad can. In school, you have to keep remembering many things in your head. In farming, when you finally do something like cut and spear a tobacco plant, it stays with you and you know it forever. So I know a lot now about how to do most everything on our farm. And none of it has been like a school lesson.

Most of our tenants through the years have shied away from much school. They've learned a lot, though, and know how to do most anything there is to do on a farm. They understand a lot about how nature is, and understand two main things. They have to be honest, and can't be afraid of work. My granddad has always tried to find tenants who are honest and who know how to work and will. You can soon tell if somebody is afraid of work. If they jump right in from the start, it's a good sign. If they stand around, it's not. If somebody around us ever shows any signs of not being honest, they don't last long. That goes for neighbors as well as tenants. If ever I've learned anything, it's to be honest, because my granddad always talks about it.

Now I do start to thinking about it when they tell the story about me when I was too little to remember. Whenever farmers have something to sell, another farmer comes and looks and studies it. If it's a horse, you just let them look at it and not tell everything about it.

You don't tell the age of the horse unless asked. Most farmers look in the horse's mouth anyway and can tell the age by the teeth. If they ask you, then you have to be honest and tell the truth, but some farmers kind of stretch the truth or don't tell it all. The man who is thinking about buying something has to decide by mostly looking at it, because the owner won't say much if there is anything the matter. Well, we had a mule for sale then, and a man came to look at it. We got rid of our mules and used only horses when I was about five, because mules are too contrary. He was looking at this mule and studying it and I don't remember, but they say I walked up and said, "You don't want that mule, because he's blind in one eye and can't see out of the other." I had heard them talk about the mule that couldn't see very good and heard somebody say what I told the man. But since I still hear the story once in a while, I've wondered about the honesty part if it all. I don't know what really went on, but I've never known my granddad to ever cheat or not be honest in every way.

As I get older, I do see people lie and cheat, and it bothers me. I wonder if there are times when you should lie. But if you lie once, then it might get easier to lie the next time. My granddad has told about the time when he lied to the law. Years ago, he had a tenant named Tom, who was a good worker and a good man and my granddad liked him, but he would get drunk every now and then. Well, Tom started making a little whiskey before he moved to our place to sell and help feed his big family, and the law came after him. They were in the barn when they saw the law coming, so Tom jumped into a pile of hay and asked my granddad to cover him up. When the law came in and asked if my granddad had seen Tom, he told them, no he hadn't.

He gave as the reasons that they would have taken Tom to jail and his big family would have nearly starved, and he thought he did the right thing. He also thought he could stop Tom from making whiskey. One of the things as you get older is that you hear about all these different things coming up in life and you see honesty twisted around a little. Now I never thought my granddad would ever do anybody wrong, and I'm sure he wouldn't. But it makes you wonder if you'll get into something where you might have to twist honesty around to do the best thing.

It's fun when the first big snow comes. It means sleigh riding and sliding across the ice on the ponds and playing in the big snowdrifts. With our long sloping hills, there are many good places to sled down and build up so much steam that you have to be very careful. Back behind the dairy barn, we have a long sloping hill that is not too steep. At the bottom is a pond, and when it freezes over and a snow comes, it is the best place to take a sled. You can go a long way and then end up scooting across the pond and put your feet out to stop. I don't sleigh-ride as much as I used to, because I have more work to do and am not as interested. I'd rather shoot ball if it is not too cold, but it has to be really cold and snowy not to go shoot ball when I have the time.

Our farm looks much different in winter. It seems so still and naked like. It looks dead and as if it will never come back to life as the winter wears on. When I walk back on the place alone, and the only sound is a cow calling far off through the cold air, it seems more peaceful than during the busy hot days of summer or the warming moist early spring days when everything is coming alive. I think of Christmas coming and when they talk so much about peace on earth and good will. Christmas is the best time of the year, so the cold, still days don't seem so bad, because we're getting ready for all the things that Christmas brings.

My granddad sends me to the other barns back on the place to feed sometimes. If a good snow has fallen during the night, when I'm walking back a ridge and down to a creek the next morning, I can see how much life there is when it all looked so dead. The tracks are everywhere, especially down by the creeks. It makes me wonder how much alive the hills really are. There are rabbit, fox, coon, muskrat, possum and sometimes mink and other tracks going all around. If I stop and stand still and listen, I might hear a rustle in the leaves under a tree where a squirrel has come out from his den to look for a bite to eat. The birds stop in the bare trees and chirp in a happy way, not minding the cold.

When the sun goes down on one of those kind of days, I like to be back on the place. I think of the warm barn where the cows are in for the night and the sheep in their barn chewing softly on their hay. The dogs and cats like to stay in the barn on winter nights, and the sparrows and pigeons dart in and out and pick the seeds that shake loose from the hay. Knowing they're safe and full and warm is a good feeling when we finally close the door at night. And I know that the stove in the kitchen is roaring and the new fresh sausage cakes are frying. That's what I mean by noticing the peace of it all.

I used to wonder during Christmas time about Jesus being born in a manger and how it could happen that way. And I would imagine our barn and where it could have happened there. I would stand out there and see the wise men and shepherds riding up one of our ridges to see him. And I've thought that maybe God planned no room in the inn, and that it would happen in a manger just to show he picked out a peaceful place where all his creatures amount to something.

Last year about the middle of December when there was a good snow on, my granddad woke me up about four in the morning and told me to walk down and get Crit and Sollie to come up and milk early. He said that Floyd had called him and told him that he could haul our tobacco to the market that day. So I walked down the ridge in the snow to their houses and beat on their doors and told them to come to milk because they had to load the tobacco. After we milked, my granddad told me to stay home from school and do all the barn work since they had to go to the tobacco warehouse.

There is a lot of barn work to do in the winter, and I knew what to do. You have to wash and clean all the milk buckets and cans, because you never know when the city inspector is coming to see if you are keeping everything clean. The cows have to be turned out in the lot and if the pond is frozen, then you have to chop holes in the ice with an old ax so they can drink. The hardest part is cleaning out the barn and all the manure and piss that the cows have dumped during the night. A big wheelbarrow full is heavy and hard to push up the ramp outside at the manure pile. A man can push a wheelbarrow full, but I have to take smaller loads, so it takes more time. Hay and silage have to be thrown down and bedding of straw scattered down for the cows when they come back in the barn. It took me most of the day to do it all, but I felt kind of proud to show that I could do it all.

My granddad has taken me to the tobacco sales a time or two. What you do is haul the stripped tobacco to the big warehouse at Paris or Lexington and then unload it on big flat baskets. You try to stack it neat and pretty so it looks good and the buyers will like it. After it's unloaded and stacked, they tell you when it will sell a few days later, so you have to go back. Sale day is the big day and you'll be either happy or a little sad. When you go, they start out with the auctioneer walking down a row and jabbering in a sing-song way that you can't understand. The buyers from the big tobacco companies walk along with him and if they like the looks of a basket, will holler out a price at the auctioneer and buy it. The farmers walk along behind them anxious and nervous, hoping for the best.

It all happens so fast. After you go to the office and get the check, sometimes the tenants and the farmers want to stop and buy some extra things and Christmas things with some of the money. Most get some bananas and oranges to take home and a little candy for the kids, so everybody gets something extra on tobacco sales day. We usually go to a restaurant to eat and it all is a treat. Tenants seldom ever get to eat in a restaurant. I remember one time my granddad had to order everything from the menu because our tenants at the time couldn't read or understand the words on the menu.

We've had a few tenants who tried to sneak off and buy a bottle of whiskey. At the tobacco market, you'll see some farmers over to the side take a pint out of their pocket and take a big swig and pass it around. I've never tasted whiskey and never thought about it much, but I've smelled it. We don't have much drinking around our neighborhood, but you do hear about more drinking around Christmas time. I guess everybody gets in a good mood and it's cold, and I've heard that a good shot of whiskey will warm you up. I know some of my uncles will drink some beer and get a bottle of whiskey now and then.

When the war was over and our boys came back, some of them got pretty wild and drank and carried on. Older people said they had been through so much fighting that they couldn't settle down. One of my uncles was tough and fought the Japs on the islands in the Pacific Ocean. When he got home, he couldn't settle down. He wouldn't say too much, but I heard that he told about when he was in a big fight and one of his buddies got wounded. My uncle picked him up and was running and carrying him away and the Japs shot his wounded buddy again right through the head while he was in my uncle's arms and trying to be carried to safety.

When I was little during the war, I didn't know enough to know what it was all about. I wasn't interested in the news on the radio and hearing about how many were killed and wounded every day. Now I can see more about how bad it was. You see and hear about some of the soldiers still having nightmares at night and smoking one cigarette after the other and drinking every day. All my four uncles who went to war made it back. My mother had several cousins who went and two never made it home. Their homes are still very sad, and they say that Christmas is going to be very hard.

Christmas shouldn't ever be a hard time. A few weeks before, you can feel all the excitement everywhere. One of the first things is when we put up our Christmas tree. My granddad used to take me with a horse and sled back the ridge to find a nice shaped cedar and we would cut it and bring it home. He'd put it in an old bucket and fix it in there so it would stand up, and we'd bring it in the living room. At school, the teachers had us cut out strips of our tablets between the lines and color them different bright colors. We'd make paper chains by gluing the strips into rings and take them home and wrap them around the tree. My mother pops a lot of popcorn, and my sister and I take a string and a big needle and make a long popcorn strand to wrap around the tree. We'd have other things to put on the tree, and when we finally got electricity, the lights make it pretty. I used to like to turn out all the lights except the tree lights and sit and look at it. The only light in the room was a little light coming from the air damper in the coal stove and the tree lights, which are so pretty. I could sit there and just think about Christmas.

The Christmas before the war ended, my granddad said that I should go cut several cedars and take them to town to give to my aunts and some of our other friends. During the war, you had to save all the money you could, and town people might have a hard time finding and getting trees. I hitched up a team to a wagon, went back on the place and cut about six or eight cedars that would make good Christmas trees and brought them to the barn. The next morning, I asked Pete our milk truck driver if he could throw them in the milk truck in a day or two and take them to town for me. Pete was always good to me, but he acted like he didn't know where to put all those Christmas trees in with all the cans of milk. He finally said he would take them, so we took them to town and unloaded them at my Aunt Fay's house. My Uncle John was fighting in the war somewhere in Germany at the time. I took the trees around to other houses and gave them away so people would have a Christmas tree. My granddad says you should help other people, and he's always doing things like that. I could see how good it was when everybody thanked me so much.

When I was little, my mother would start looking for some boxes at the mailbox along about the middle of December. There would be several big boxes coming from Sears and Roebuck, and she would never open them in December when my sister or I were around. Of course, we were excited about Santa Claus coming, but I remember starting to think that she might be getting our toys from Sears and Roebuck and Santa wasn't actually bringing them. I couldn't see how it all worked out with Santa Claus coming down our chimney into the fire. When I was pretty sure that there wasn't a real Santa Claus who watched to see if you were good, one of my uncles told me that Santa would actually come and look in your window to check on you. One night he was at our house and he went outside when we weren't looking. Suddenly, there was a banging on the window and it scared me. We ran over and I looked out and really thought I saw Santa drive away into the sky. Then I knew he was real.

At school, we put up a tree in each room. The little kids color all kinds of Christmas pictures to put up on the wall. We also draw names and give a little present to the name you draw. The teachers know that some poor kids can't buy a present, so they bring extra presents and kind of slip them into the pile after checking to see if everyone has something with his name on it. They try to keep it a secret, but you know what they're doing. It's fun to draw names, but I can see that some of the tenant kids and poor kids never get much of anything anytime. Maybe some of them get one present or two. All the excitement keeps building up, but I've stopped to think about the poor kids. They don't get as excited as we do, and I've been a little sad thinking about it. I've actually heard a tenant farmer say that Christmas doesn't mean that much to him, and then you think of his kids.

At church, we start singing Christmas carols and practicing for the Christmas program a couple of weeks before. A week or two before that, somebody at church gets up and makes a motion that the church give a treat to all the kids in the area whether they go to church or not. At the store, Elmer and May fix many sacks and put in an orange and an apple, some hard candy, some chocolate drops, some kisses and a few peanuts still in the hull. I've taken some of these sacks to the tenant kids, and they are always excited and glad.

Everything about my life changes as I get older. I sometimes liked it better the old way when I wasn't worrying about growing up to be a man. It seems like there's something in me that pushes me on and then something else holding me back. It all seemed so happy when I think back to when I would take the sack of treats from the Christmas program at church and hold it so tight and not want to eat it all at once. I tried to keep something in it for a long time so that it would never be all gone. Now I know that you have to go on and more things are put on you, and some of them are happy and some are not.

A year or two ago, I was thinking about what play-things and games I would get for Christmas. Now I've got five ewes of my own, and they will soon be lambing. It's like I'm being pushed, and I don't rightly know if I'm ready to get into it all or want to. I can see that one of the biggest changes is how I look at Christmas. When you believe in Santa Claus, it's like everything is magic and exciting. You think about the North Pole and the sky and how Santa could land on your roof. It's hard to give up believing in magical things, but I now know there's no magic to anything.

The way it was when I was little was that my granddad would have to go milk before we could get up and run to the Christmas tree. My uncle, aunt and cousin Sue would come out from town on Christmas Eve and stay with us. My sister, Sue and I could hardly wait in the bed until we heard my granddad come in from the barn. Now I have to go help milk before we open the presents, but I still get a little excited about it. It's what leads up to it all that makes it a wonderful time.

This year, we practiced for a little play at church to put on the Sunday night before Christmas. I was a little nervous about getting up on the platform where the preacher preaches. I had to remember what to say and was acting like a newspaper boy selling papers telling about the good news of Christmas. When we were ready to go to the program, my mother brought out a present and told me to open it. I did, and it was a green sweater with white reindeer all over. I put it on and we went to the program. I felt so good wearing the new green sweater. It made me feel like I looked nice, and I thought that the people watching me would also think I looked nice. It was a cold clear night and the stars were very bright. The fresh snow cover made the whole country look peaceful, and I could imagine everything about the warm manger and the shepherds going there. It all made me feel like I knew it really did happen with Christ actually being born and living. Everything was like it was coming together to make me understand more about how good the whole world is.

At church, they turned off most of the lights for the Christmas program and lit candles at the window sills. The tree up in the corner still had its lights on and it looked so pretty. We started out with singing carols for a while and then had a solo or two and some prayers in between. Before the preacher told about Christmas, which was more like a story than a sermon, he had John Wilson get up and read about the story of the birth of Jesus from the Bible. John stammered around and was probably nervous like I was before I had to get up there.

After that, the little kids got up and said verses and sang, and then we put on the play. When it was time for me to come out, I was scared at first, but then settled down, and I think it was my new green sweater that made me feel kind of proud. I walked out there and never missed a word, and when it was over, I felt like the people liked me. It was a real good feeling. They then passed out the sacks of treats for all the kids and it was over.

We only live about a mile and a half from the Short Creek Baptist Church, and you can see it from our house. It is up on a high ridge and our house is up on a ridge with rolling hills in between. It stands there every day like it is looking back at us. We hear the same thing about Christmas every year and read the same verses from the New Testament about the birth. I guess my favorite part is about when the shepherds came. I know how they have to be with their sheep and what they have to do.

When we drove home, I held the sack of treats in my hand and looked out the car window. Everything seemed even more peaceful as we passed over the ridges and hills. I don't know what it was or what caused it, but I had a good feeling about everything. When we got home and swept the snow off our shoes on the back porch and went in, the wood stove in the kitchen was still plenty warm. My granddad goes to bed real early, so he went upstairs to his room, but soon came back down with his work clothes on. He told my mother that he'd better go check on the sheep, and that's all he said. Although they weren't ready to start lambing for another week or two, some could start lambing early.

He put on his old coat and hat and went out to the porch and lit a lantern. I stood by the kitchen window and could see out through the yard and past the pear tree and past the dairy barn and all the way past the pond and up to the tobacco barn where the sheep were resting for the night. The stars and snow gave off enough light to make it so you could see it all standing there in the quiet. It was a different kind of night, and I don't know what made it so. The cows and the sheep and all were in for the night and I was warm and the only sound was the little crackling of the flames in the stove. Everything seemed good and safe and warm, and I stood there and wondered about many things all kind of jammed together. I even wondered if the cows and sheep and horses somehow knew that it was Christmas time. I always give them a little extra crushed corn on Christmas day so they too get a present.

I could see the lantern light waving gently as he walked away. The light got dimmer as he neared the barn. It stopped at the door, but then it moved again ever so slightly. He must have been in the barn and closed the door when the light went out. I knew he was in there with his sheep. It's where he wanted to be, and I believe they knew he would come.

This is the 1946-47 Goforth Green Devils basketball team and cheerleaders. We made a court outside and sewed green numbers on our undershirts. It was a good team.

This is my great-grandfather Frank W. Conrad with some of his grandchildren and great-grandchildren. I'm the one at the bottom on the left.

Some of our sheep out by the barn lot.

My good friend Eddie and me are ready to go to town.

My granddad with a good Hampshire buck out by the corn crib.

My granddad with some sheep by a rail fence.

Our milk cows taking a bath as the city woman said.

A couple of hands cutting and spearing tobacco.

My sister out by the yard gate.

Some of our sheep down by Sollie's house.

Our house where we live.

Our Short Creek Baptist Church.

One of my little cousins and me on Dolly the work mare.

My mother, sister and me and my dad when we were all together.

My granddad, sister and me ready to go to church. We took most of
our pictures when we dressed up.

Sheep out at pasture, and you can see how our hills are.

I'm loading a can of milk on Pete's truck.

Two of my cousins on Lady with my granddad who couldn't do
without her.

My granddad is ready for church. You can see my basketball goal on
the barn with the burlap sack for a net.

My 7th grade picture. I had a Red Cross button on, because I donated to help people.

My sister and my mother and me when I was about six before the war.

About the Author


Terry Cummins ran his first marathon at age 63, technically climbed his first mountain at age 64 and wrote his first book at age 68. Better late than never works for him. He left the farm at age 18 to go to college, and never returned to live there as was intended. The farm never left him. FEED MY SHEEP is his way of going back to that vibrant life during his 13th year in 1947. After college, the military and 34 years in public education primarily as a secondary school administrator, he retired and lives in New Albany, Indiana. In addition to writing a weekly newspaper commentary on various topics, other marathons, mountains and books are in his future plans.

Printed in the United States
1488500005B/142-303